Why do you do what you do?

Why do you get out of bed in the morning?

And why should anyone care?

It is one of life's greatest joys to wake up in the morning

      Every morning

with a clear sense of why the day matters

      Why every day matters.

This is what it means to find your Why.

It is the start of an inspiring journey

      Your inspiring journey.

PORTFOLIO / PENGUIN

FIND YOUR WHY

SIMON SINEK is an optimist who believes in a brighter future for humanity. His talk on TED.com is the third most watched talk of all time. Learn more about his work and how you can inspire those around you at StartWithWhy.com.

ALSO BY SIMON SINEK

Start with Why:
How Great Leaders Inspire Everyone to Take Action

Leaders Eat Last:
Why Some Teams Pull Together and Others Don't

Together Is Better:
A Little Book of Inspiration
(illustrated by Ethan M. Aldridge)
The Infinite Game

DAVID MEAD began as a corporate trainer. In 2009, he joined the Start With Why team to develop content to help Simon share his powerful ideas. Now he speaks and facilitates workshops to help shift people's perceptions about leadership and culture.

PETER DOCKER is a former senior Royal Air Force officer and professional pilot. Since joining the Start With Why team in 2011, Peter has worked with organizations around the world to help them articulate their purpose, educate their leaders and to create cultures where each individual thrives.

FIND YOUR WHY

A PRACTICAL GUIDE FOR DISCOVERING PURPOSE FOR YOU AND YOUR TEAM

Simon Sinek

with David Mead and Peter Docker

PORTFOLIO / PENGUIN

PORTFOLIO / PENGUIN
An imprint of Penguin Random House LLC
375 Hudson Street
New York, New York 10014
penguin.com

Most Portfolio books are available at a discount when purchased in quantity for sales promotions or corporate use. Special editions, which include personalized covers, excerpts, and corporate imprints, can be created when purchased in large quantities. For more information, please call (212) 572-2232 or e-mail specialmarkets@penguinrandomhouse.com. Your local bookstore can also assist with discounted bulk purchases using the Penguin Random House corporate Business-to-Business program. For assistance in locating a participating retailer, e-mail B2B@penguinrandomhouse.com.

LIBRARY OF CONGRESS CATALOGING-IN-PUBLICATION DATA
Names: Sinek, Simon, author.
Title: Find your why / Simon Sinek with David Mead and Peter Docker.
Description: New York, New York : Portfolio/Penguin, an imprint of
    Penguin Random House, LLC, [2017]
Identifiers: LCCN 2017019047 (print) | LCCN 2017023567 (ebook) |
    ISBN 9781101992982 (ebook) | ISBN 9780143111726 (pbk.)
Subjects: LCSH: Attitude (Psychology) | Optimism. | Conduct of life.
Classification: LCC BF327 (ebook) | LCC BF327 .S56 2017 (print) |
    DDC 152.4—dc23
LC record available at https://lccn.loc.gov/2017019047

Printed in the United States of America
10

CONTENTS

by Simon Sinek

Fulfillment is a right and not a privilege. Every single one of us is entitled to feel fulfilled by the work we do, to wake up feeling inspired to go to work, to feel safe when we're there and to return home with a sense that we contributed to something larger than ourselves. Fulfillment is not a lottery. It is not a feeling reserved for a lucky few who get to say, "I love what I do."

For those who hold a leadership position, creating an environment in which the people in your charge feel like they are a part of something bigger than themselves is your responsibility as a leader. For those who work for an organization that does not leave you feeling inspired at the beginning and end of every day, you must become the leader you wish you had. Regardless of our rank in the organization, every single one of us has at least one colleague, client or vendor for whom we can take some responsibility for how they feel when they work with us. The goal is not to focus on what's standing in your way; it is to take steps that will have a positive and lasting effect on everyone around us.

The concept of WHY is a deeply personal journey born out of pain. I discovered the idea at a time when I had lost any passion for my work. The advice people gave me wasn't helpful either: "Do what you love," "Find your bliss," "Be passionate." All accurate—but totally un-actionable. I agreed with all the advice in theory, but I didn't know what to change. I didn't know what to do differently on Monday. And that's the reason the WHY has been and continues to be such a profound force in my life. Not only did discovering my WHY renew my passion, it gave me a filter to make better decisions. It offered me a new lens through which I would see the world differently. And it was through this lens—to inspire people to do what inspires them so that together each of us can change our world—that I started preaching the concept of WHY and the Golden Circle. And people listened. In fact, people did more than listen, they joined me in preaching this message, sharing the vision. And our movement was born.

The TED Talk I gave in 2009 helped spread the idea to more people, and my first book, *Start with Why*, made the case for WHY in much greater depth. People and organizations who know their WHY enjoy greater, long-term success, command greater trust and loyalty among employees and customers and are more forward-thinking and innovative than their competition. The concept of WHY and the Golden Circle became a huge piece of the puzzle to advance this world I imagined. But there was a problem.

Though I was able to make the case for the existence and the power of WHY, and though I could help some people and organizations discover their WHY, I wasn't able to get to or help as many people as we needed to if we are to have an impact in lots of people's lives. My team built upon what I started. They made my process even better. They started helping people. They even developed an online course to help people discover their WHY. But even that wasn't enough.

That's the reason this book exists. If *Start with Why* makes the case for the WHY, *Find Your Why* provides the steps to show people how to actually do it. And just as *Start with Why* illustrates, though I may be the guy with the idea, I don't know how to bring it to life at scale. That's where David and Peter come in.

Peter Docker and David Mead joined me on this journey because they were inspired by the world I imagined. Both have a unique skill set to help bring my vision—*our* vision—to reality. I may have figured out how to help one person learn their WHY, but it was David and Peter that figured out how to help a room of sixty people, for example, find their WHY.

David knows how to make things work. Years ago, inspired by one of my talks, he started developing workbooks and building training programs to help the people at his then-company. He did this without ever asking me or anyone else for help. Once I got wind of what he had done, I was blown away by how deeply he understood my ideas and his ability to put them into practice.

Peter retired from the Royal Air Force and wanted to continue a life of service in the private sector. He discovered my work and reached out to simply say how much it inspired him. He has combined my ideas with work he was already doing to amplify its impact. Soon after we met, he started mentoring folks on our team just out of the goodness of his own heart. His work was so good that we started using many of his ideas to help build our company and grow our movement.

Both eventually joined our team and a deep friendship formed between the two of them. Their collective genius has taken my work and made it even better. So when the opportunity came to write a follow-up guide to *Start with Why*, I turned to David and Peter to help. These guys are the "how" to my "why." And I love that our movement has given them the ability to share their expertise with so many more people.

This book has been years in the making. Peter and David have traveled the world to talk about the WHY and work closely with individuals and organizations to help them understand, discover and use the concepts. They have heard the questions, discovered the roadblocks and found better and better ways to advance the vision. And that's where you come in.

If we are to profoundly change the way in which the business world works, if we help organizations create cultures in which trust and cooperation are the norm rather than the exception, if we are to build the world we imagine, we will need help. Lots of it. Though the work my team is doing is making a dent, we alone will be unable to create the kind of change necessary. It will take an army.

David and Peter wrote this book to be a practical guide. A complete self-contained handbook that gives any person the pieces they need to discover and articulate their WHY. We designed the book with lots of space in the margins so that you can take notes along the way. Fill in the blanks, dog-ear the pages, highlight as you go. Don't be precious about it.

Find Your Why is a journey. Though all the how-to steps may be in the book, it's going to take work and patience to really get it. Remember, this book is a guide. Follow the steps, learn the concepts and absolutely tweak as you go to make the process your own. If you find something that works better for you, do it!

Think of this book as the gun that fires at the beginning of the race. That bang fills you with excitement and energy as you set off. But it is the lessons you will learn as you run the race—as you learn to live your WHY—that will inspire you and show you what you are capable of. And remember the most important lesson. The goal is not simply for you to cross the finish line, but to see how many people you can inspire to run with you.

There is an entire section in the bookshop called "self-help," but there is no section called "help-others." This is what we are all doing together—we are pioneering the help-others industry. For all of the people who want to learn their WHY, who want their companies to start with WHY, who want to help others find their WHY . . . for all of the people who want to help build a world in which the vast majority of people wake up inspired to go to work, to feel safe when they are there and to return home fulfilled by the work they do . . . I say welcome. The more of us who raise our hands and say, "Count me in," the greater the chance that we will build the world we imagine. You in?

FIND YOUR WHY

INTRODUCTION

We travel a lot for business, but sometimes our business just won't wait—it climbs right onto the plane and finds us. That's what happened to Peter one day, on a flight from Miami to St. Louis. Here's the story as Peter tells it:

I was exhausted. All I wanted to do was get to where I was going. Another flight. Another stranger to sit next to. I prayed to the airline gods for a seatmate who wouldn't invade my space, physically or verbally. I just wanted to be left alone. But as it turned out, my neighbor *was* going to be one of those people and this *was* going to be one of those flights.

I was settling in for the four-hour trip when Steve sat down and introduced himself. After some chitchat, he started telling me what he does for a living. If you've been in this situation, you already know that Steve was not, say, a bodyguard for Hollywood stars, eager to share behind-the-scenes stories about their love lives and recreational drug use. No salacious stories or gossip to entertain me for the flight. No. For twenty-three years, Steve had been selling steel. Yup, steel. Riveting.

It turns out, however, the steel Steve sells is not just the run-of-the-mill variety. His company, based in Sweden, produces a particularly pure form of steel that enables machines to run more efficiently because their parts—for example, a car's transmission—are lighter. An engineer himself, Steve could personally attest to his product's superiority over other options on the market.

As he wrapped up, Steve looked at me expectantly, obviously longing for a follow-up question that would let him talk more about steel. Trouble was, I didn't much care what Steve did. It's not that I'm aloof or unsociable or only interested in gossip. I'm none of the above. What draws me in is not *what* people do for a living but *why* they do it. So instead of asking Steve how much his steel costs and who his best clients are, I turned to him and said, "So what?"

"Well, er," Steve faltered, not understanding the question. So I put it another way: "I get that the steel you sell is very pure. I get that it allows for lighter components, which makes machines more efficient. But so what?"

Steve stammered a bit more, then blurted out, "Well, not so much material needs to be used."

Getting closer, I pushed a little more.

"And what difference does that make?" For a moment Steve looked as if he might crumble. All he'd wanted was to make small talk. Now he was stuck with my weird questions for the next three hours (the tables had turned). But we kept talking and I helped him find his answers.

As it turns out, such pure steel means that parts built with less material still remain strong. Using less material means needing to do less smelting (the process of extracting metal from its ore), so less energy is used in the steel production process and thus less pollution is created. And when the steel is used to produce a machine such as a car, those advantages are repeated: the car is lighter, so it uses less fuel and therefore produces less pollution. And as if that weren't enough, purer steel is easier to recycle than other varieties. This was actually interesting . . . but we still hadn't gotten to why Steve was so enthusiastic about his job.

"Saving fuel and reducing pollution is great," I said, "but there must be something more to this business that's kept you going for twenty-three years." That's a long time to do something and still be passionate about it. "There must be something more at stake, something you truly believe in," I prodded him. And then it happened. For the first time in our conversation, I saw Steve's eyes light up. And his feelings poured out.

Steve is committed to keeping the planet healthy for his children and future generations, and one way to do that is to be more responsible in the way we use our planet's rich resources. For all the time he'd been talking to me about steel, he never once mentioned this, yet it was the very thing that inspired him to start telling a stranger on a plane all about pure steel.

I asked Steve for permission to rephrase his sales pitch. "In simple terms," I began, speaking as if I were Steve, "I believe in using natural resources for the benefit of humankind. And I also believe that we should do so responsibly, leaving the planet safe and healthy for our children. This is what led me to become an engineer and to join my current organization. Our company, based in Sweden—a country committed to sustainability—has developed a way to help engineers create lighter, more efficient, greener products. And our particular path to sustainability happens to be lightweight steel."

"Thank you," Steve said, beaming. "You've just put into words the reason I love what I do."

Simply by starting my version of the pitch with *why* he loves his job, I helped Steve see that it's not *what* he does that has kept him fulfilled for more than two decades. What inspires him is *why* he does it. By connecting his work to his sense of purpose, Steve had discovered his WHY.

* * *

Your vision is only actionable if you say it out loud. If you keep it to yourself, it will remain a figment of your imagination.

_____

Every one of us has a WHY, a deep-seated purpose, cause or belief that is the source of our passion and inspiration. You may not yet know what yours is or how to express it in words. But we guarantee, you have one. If you'd like to understand your WHY, and would rather not wait until Peter sits next to you on a flight, this book can help. We believe that all of us deserve to live as Steve does: waking up inspired to go to work and coming home, at the end of the day, feeling fulfilled by the work we do.

Fulfillment isn't another word for happiness. All kinds of things make us happy at work: hitting a goal, getting a promotion, landing a new client, completing a project—the list goes on. But happiness is temporary; the feeling doesn't last. Nobody walks around energized by the memory of a goal hit twelve months ago. That intensity passes with time.

Fulfillment is deeper. Fulfillment lasts. The difference between happiness and fulfillment is the difference between liking something and loving something. We don't necessarily *like* our kids all the time, for example, but we do *love* them all the time. We don't necessarily find happiness in our jobs every day, but we can feel fulfilled by our work every day if it makes us feel part of something bigger than ourselves. (That's the reason we can feel *un*fulfilled even if we're successful by standard measures like compensation and status. Fulfillment comes when our job connects directly to our WHY.) Steve, our man of steel, finds *happi-*

ness when he closes a deal but finds *fulfillment* knowing that he is contributing to a higher cause with larger implications. Happiness comes from *what* we do. Fulfillment comes from *why* we do it.

Steve is a lucky man. Though he couldn't articulate his WHY until he met and talked with Peter, he had been *living* his WHY for decades and as a result felt inspired and fulfilled. But what if the company in Sweden had been acquired by a larger company that downsized Steve? What if he'd had to look for a new job without knowing his WHY? Given his decades of experience, he'd most likely have tried for another job selling steel. But if the new company wasn't dedicated to sustainability, his sense of purpose would have vanished along with his enthusiasm when talking to strangers on planes. And he might never have connected the pieces and seen that his passion for his work actually had nothing to do with steel in the first place.

If we want to feel an undying passion for our work, if we want to feel we are contributing to something bigger than ourselves, we all need to know our WHY. And that's the reason we wrote this book.

* * *

Find Your Why is a distillation of what our team has learned from over twenty-five years of collective experience conducting Why Discoveries. We have helped all kinds of people—including entrepreneurs, individual employees, small businesses and teams within large businesses—to find their WHY. This book was designed to help you find yours.

Below is an outline of the seven chapters. The first two contain information that's fundamental to finding your WHY, and we urge everyone to read them. After that, you can move on to either chapter 3 or chapter 4, depending on whether you're discovering your WHY as an individual or as a team or group member. Finally, we recommend that all readers review chapters 5, 6 and 7. At the end of the book, we offer assorted bits of additional information that may help you as questions arise.

- Chapter 1 is a highly condensed recap of *Start with Why*, the book written by Simon Sinek, who popularized the concept of WHY. This section discusses some of the benefits of knowing your WHY.

- Chapter 2 provides an overview of the process of discovering your WHY. This is important to read whether you're doing this on your own or with a team.

- Chapter 3 is the step-by-step process for individuals—entrepreneurs or employees—to find their personal WHY. If you are using this book to help your team or organization find its WHY, though not imperative, completing this section and learning your own WHY can help you lead your group through the discovery process.

- Chapter 4 explains what you need to do to prepare for a Why Discovery for a team, organization or any "tribe" in which people are brought together to work.

- Chapter 5 picks up where chapter 4 leaves off and explains how to take a tribe through the Why Discovery process.

- The WHY is the destination and HOWs are the route we take to get there. Chapter 6 is all about the HOWs, the actions we take to bring our WHY to life.

- Chapter 7 explains how to share your WHY with others, and how to begin to live your WHY and put it into practice.

- The appendixes provide answers to the questions we receive most often in our workshops and "cheat sheets" for when you (or another facilitator) are conducting the workshops.

One of the hardest things to predict about finding your WHY is how long it will take. In chapters 3 through 5, we outline the process for individuals and tribes, and estimate, based on our experience, *approximately* how much time each step will take. But these numbers are only averages. For some, the process goes more quickly, and for others, more slowly. There is no "right" amount of time. What's important is to stick with each section or step until you feel confident about moving on to the next one.

To be honest, knowing you're about to turn the page to chapter 1, we feel a little jealous. We love helping people find their WHY. For us—Peter and David—we wish we could be there personally with each one of you. But our vision is to bring the WHY to life for as many people as possible. And so we will be your virtual guides as you set off on your adventure. Inspire on!

Start with Why

A Primer

Sometimes a project that looks like an easy win for us turns into a disappointment or even a disaster. More importantly, sometimes we, or a competitor, succeed brilliantly when all the usual business assumptions say we should have flopped. These outcomes can seem mysterious, but they're not if looked at in a framework that starts with WHY.

In his book, *Start with Why*, Simon Sinek uses a model that he calls the Golden Circle to explain how legendary leaders such as Steve Jobs, Martin Luther King Jr. and the Wright brothers were able to achieve what others who were just as smart and hardworking, and sometimes better funded, were not.

If you've read Simon's book or seen him talk about WHY on TED.com (http://bit.ly/GoldenCircleTalk), you're already familiar with the Golden Circle; this chapter will serve to remind you of the most important points. If the Golden Circle is new for you, what follows is the heart of the matter—and is essential preparation for your own search for WHY.

Every organization—and every person's career—operates on three levels, as shown in the illustration on the next page: *What* we do, *how* we do it, and *why* we do it. We all know *what* we do: the products we sell, the services we offer or the jobs we do. Some of us know *how* we do it: the things that we think make us different or stand out from

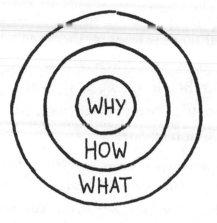

the crowd. But very few of us can clearly articulate *why* we do what we do.

"Hold on," you might say. "Let's be honest here—aren't most people working to earn money? That's the obvious 'why.'" First, money is a result. Though it is a part of the picture, it's not what inspires any one of us to get out of bed in the morning. And for the cynics out there who think they or others really do get out of bed for the money, the question we ask is, what is the reason they want the money. Is it for freedom? To travel? To provide a lifestyle for their kids that they didn't have? Is it to keep score and show they have done more than others? The point is, money isn't the thing that drives people. WHY goes much deeper to understanding what motivates and inspires us. It is the purpose, cause or belief that drives every organization and every person's individual career. *Why* does your company exist? *Why* did you get out of bed this morning? And *why* should anyone care?

When we meet new customers or clients, the first thing most of us tell them is *what* we do. Then we explain *how* we do it or *how* we are different. This, we think, will be enough to win their business, sway their point of view or convince them to take a particular action. The following pitch follows that template:

We sell paper. We offer the highest quality product at the best possible price. Lower than any of our competitors. Wanna buy some?

This is a very rational pitch. It states clearly what the company does and attempts to persuade potential buyers to choose its product over others' on the basis of features and benefits. Though this approach may work now and then, at best it will result in a few recurring transactions. As soon as the buyer finds a better deal, they will be gone, because the pitch doesn't differentiate this specific vendor from other companies in any way that truly matters. Loyalty is not built on features and benefits. Features and benefits do not inspire. Loyalty and long-lasting relationships are based on something deeper.

Let's try the pitch again. Let's start with WHY:

What good is an idea if it can't be shared? Our company was founded to help spread ideas. The more ideas that are shared, the greater the likelihood those ideas will have an impact in the world. There are many ways to share ideas; one is the written word. That's where we come in. We make paper for those words. We make paper for big ideas. Wanna buy some?

Totally different, right? Starting with WHY just made paper sound really good. And if it can do that for a commodity, imagine what it can do for a product that really can stand out. This pitch is not based on facts and figures, features and benefits. Those things have value but not first. Leading with WHY has a deeper, more emotional and ultimately more influential value. When we use the second pitch, we're no longer talking about paper. We're talking about who our company is and what we stand for. Of course, you'll always get those people who just want a ream of paper. And yet, if your customers' personal beliefs and values align with those expressed in your pitch—i.e., if they believe in the spread of ideas—then they are much more likely to want to do business with you, *not just one time, but over and over and over again.* In fact, they are more likely to stay loyal even if another vendor offers a better price. It says something about them when they do business with a company that reflects their beliefs.

Companies that inspire, companies that command trust and loyalty over the long term, are the ones that make us feel we're accomplishing something bigger than just saving a buck. That feeling of alliance with something bigger is the reason we keep wearing the jersey of our hometown sports team even though they've missed the playoffs for ten years and counting. It's why some of us will always buy Apple products over other brands, even if Apple isn't always the most affordable choice. Whether we like to admit it or not, we are not entirely rational beings. If we were, no one would ever fall in love and no one would ever start a business. Faced with an overwhelming chance of failure, no rational person would ever take either of those risks. But we do. Every day. Because how we feel about something or someone is more powerful than what we think about it or them.

There's just one problem with feelings. They can be tremendously difficult to express in words. That's the reason we so often resort to metaphors and analogies, like "Our relationship feels like a train heading at high speed toward a rickety bridge." "When I get to the office, I feel like a little kid on the playground again." Even though communicating our feelings is hard, the payoff is big. When we align emotionally with our customers and clients, our connection is much stronger and more meaningful than any affiliation based on features and benefits. That's what starting with WHY is all about.

And here's the best part: This is not our opinion. This whole concept of WHY is grounded in the tenets of biology of human decision making. How the Golden Circle works maps perfectly with how our brain works.

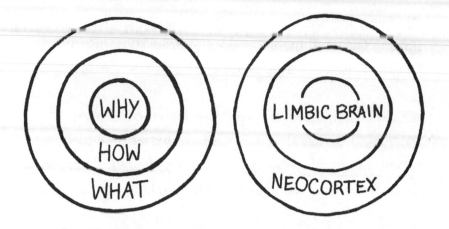

The outer section of the Golden Circle—the WHAT—corresponds to the outer section of the brain—the neocortex. This is the part of the brain responsible for rational and analytical thought. It helps us understand facts and figures, features and benefits. The neocortex is also responsible for language.

The middle two sections of the Golden Circle—the WHY and HOW—correspond to the middle section of the brain, the limbic system. This is the part of the brain responsible for all our behavior and decision making. It's also responsible for all our feelings, like trust and loyalty. But unlike the neocortex, the limbic system has no capacity for language. This is where "gut feelings" come from. It's not our stomach. It's a feeling we get about a decision we have to make that we struggle to explain.

That separation of powers is the biological reason we sometimes find it difficult to put our feelings into words

("I love you more than words can say"), explain our actions ("The devil made me do it!") or justify our decisions ("I don't know . . . it just felt right").

We can learn, however, to put words to those feelings. And those who do are the ones who are better able to inspire action in themselves, among their colleagues and with their customers. We wrote this book to help you find those words.

Once you understand your WHY, you'll be able to clearly articulate what makes you feel fulfilled and to better understand what drives your behavior when you're at your natural best. When you can do that, you'll have a point of reference for everything you do going forward. You'll be able to make more intentional choices for your business, your career and your life. You'll be able to inspire others to buy from you, work with you and join your cause. Never again should you have to play the lottery and act on gut decisions that are made for reasons you don't really understand. From now on, you will work with purpose, on purpose. From now on, you'll start with WHY.

The opportunity is not to discover the perfect company for ourselves. The opportunity is to build the perfect company for each other.

——

What WHY Looks Like in Action

The HR director, dressed in a crisp, gray business suit, looked up at Emily and barked his standard opening question: "So, what can you bring to our company?"

A few months before she graduated from college, Emily applied for a position at a large global corporation. A straight-A student who had gone to university on a full scholarship, she easily made it through the first cut and now found herself in a panel interview, where she sat across the table from the HR director and three other executives. They could see from her application that she was bright, but they worried about her lack of real-world experience. More important, they wanted to find out if she would fit their culture and how she would cope under pressure.

The man in gray elaborated: "We have a lot of highly qualified applicants for this position. Tell us what you have that they don't."

A conscientious student, Emily had prepared for the interview by learning everything she could about the company. But every other candidate had access to the same information. So Emily went a step further. Emily unleashed her WHY.

"Before I talk about what I might be able to bring to your company," she calmly told the HR director, "let me first give the reason I get out of bed every day.

"I strive to help people be the best version of themselves. That's what inspires me. Based on your website, I sense that this is precisely what you believe in too. So, why wouldn't I apply to be part of your organization?"

That caught their attention.

The interviewers stopped shuffling their papers and looked her in the face. Emily then segued to a more traditional pitch about her skills and strengths, but the battle was already won. That first exchange, which lasted less than thirty seconds, had already persuaded the interviewers to hire her. By starting with her WHY, Emily had spoken directly to the limbic, decision-making centers of their brains. By showing who she was, not just what she could do, she formed an instant and genuine connection. That's all it took. They knew in their gut that they wanted her on their team.

It was relatively straightforward for Emily too. Instead of using prep time to come up with clever answers to a host of hypothetical questions, she'd focused on being comfortable with communicating her WHY. Once she faced the panel, all she had to do was speak "from her heart" (i.e., her limbic brain) about what inspired her to want to work there. The rest of the interview felt much more like a conversation than an inquisition and all her answers validated the panelists' intuition. Afterward, her cell phone rang before she even got home. It was the HR director offering her the job.

Tools can be used for many purposes. With a hammer, for example, we can simply hang a picture or we can build a whole house. Our WHY is an equally versatile tool, with applications both narrow and broad. We can use it to ace an interview or inspire our team. An entrepreneur can use it to guide a single new venture or to direct their entire organization. A company can use it to inspire a marketing campaign or to transform its corporate culture. One tool, many uses.

Another way to think of the WHY is as a piece of a jigsaw puzzle. When you know what your piece looks like, it's much easier to see where it fits or doesn't fit. Decisions can be made more quickly and with greater certainty. And when others can see your piece, they can see whether it fits with theirs. If it does, that's when the image starts to take shape. In the real world, that looks like a team coming together to advance a common vision (or, like the people who hired Emily, knowing who to invite to join their team).

There are two ways to build a career or a business. We can go through life hunting and pecking, looking for opportunities or customers, hoping that something connects. Or we can go through life with intention, knowing what our piece looks like, knowing our WHY, and going straight to the places we fit.

Finding the Right Fit

It was break time for a group of senior TV execs going through the Why Discovery process for their company. As everyone else made a beeline for the coffee, Susan, the HR director, walked over to her colleague Jim. "I don't think we should hire him," she said.

For several weeks, Susan and Jim had been debating whether or not to hire a candidate for a critical position. They had conducted a wide search and narrowed down their short list to just one person. On paper, he looked great. He had all the boxes checked. But something just didn't feel right.

"I didn't know what the problem was before," Susan said. "But now it's so clear."

Jim finished her thought. "He doesn't believe what we believe."

Thanks to the Why Discovery process, Susan and Jim had experienced the same epiphany. The candidate in question had all the right qualifications, but he was missing something incredibly important. He couldn't champion their WHY. He was up for a key role and leaving the position empty for another few months would absolutely hurt the company. But they resolved then and there, right next to the snack table, that regardless of any short-term pain they might suffer, they would keep looking until they found someone who could do the job *and* would be the right fit for their company.

It's easier to hire someone based on their résumé. It's harder to hire someone for their cultural fit. The reason is pretty obvious. We usually hire because we have a job that needs to be done. We look at the résumé to see if the candidate has the skills and experience to do that job. Facts are involved. For better or for worse, hiring for cultural fit is usually less about facts and more about how it feels. Irresponsible executives will ignore that feeling (a.k.a. their gut) whereas good executives will listen to it. The problem is, it's still a feeling.

The WHY exists on a macro level and a micro level. A company has a WHY, each division or team has a WHY, and every individual has a WHY. The opportunity is to make sure the right people are working in the right places in the right company. We'll cover more about this idea, called Nested WHYs, in chapter 4.

In the case of the TV executives, their gut feeling that the candidate was wrong for their company, even though his skills were right, was strong enough to cause them concern. But their inability to articulate the reason they felt he was wrong kept them from using their gut feeling as the basis for making the decision. This happens to the best of us—when all signs say "go," yet our gut is telling us to hold back. It's because we are about to make a decision that's out of alignment with our values and beliefs. As soon as a company's WHY is put into words, the culture becomes a little more tangible and the right decision becomes clear immediately.

It would be nice if business was purely science, but it isn't. While some parts of a business are predictable, tangible and easy to measure (think profit, revenues and expenses), the fact is, there are huge parts of a business that are unpredictable, intangible and hard to measure (think vision, inspiration, trust . . . and hiring someone to fit the culture). It's not that we don't understand the value of the intangibles; it's that we have trouble explaining what that value is. Sometimes the intangible values are abandoned because the internal or external pressure to "make the numbers" overwhelms concerns about the company's long-term well-being. Or sometimes intangibles get ignored because we lack the ability to fully grasp or explain them, to have the patience to nurture them or to know which yardstick would accurately measure them. If we had the right tools to manage the intangibles, we'd probably give them more attention.

Tools help us keep track of inventory inside a company, but what tool can help us gauge the cultural fit of a potential employee? We can easily calculate profit by deducting our expenses from our income, but how do we accurately measure the discretionary effort of our workforce? We can know a customer's purchase history, but how do we know if they trust the company? Having no answers to these questions is the reason too many companies hire for skills before fit, talk about culture but don't know how to build it and fail to create deep, human connections with their employees and customers.

The WHY is a tool that can bring clarity to that which is fuzzy and make tangible that which is abstract. Used properly, it can be used to hire, to develop strategies and to communicate more clearly (internally and externally). The WHY can help set a vision to inspire people. The WHY can guide us to act with purpose, on purpose.

In the next few chapters, we will explain how to find your WHY and put it into words.

CHAPTER 2

Discover Your WHY

An Overview

The work world is tough: Wake up, go to work, deal with the boss (or if you are the boss, deal with everyone), make money (ideally to make more this year than last year), come home, manage personal life, go to bed, wake up, repeat. That's plenty to deal with every day. Why get fancy (and waste time) by trying to also understand *why* you do what you do? The answer to that question isn't fancy; it's simple. Whether you're reading this as an entrepreneur, an employee, as a leader of a team or a division or you want to tackle the WHY of your entire organization, discovering the WHY injects passion into our work. This is not a formula for success. There are many ways to be successful (by traditional metrics); however, the Golden Circle is a tool to help us achieve long-term, fulfilling success.

- **If you're an entrepreneur,** discover your WHY so you can communicate what is singular about your company to your employees and clients or customers. For example, Apple may not always sell the very best products— ahem, *battery life*—but if you're someone who wants to "Think Different," you probably swear by Apple on an emotional level you'd never experience with, say, Dell. And knowing your WHY makes it easier to hire the right people. Every entrepreneur wants a staff of true believers, but how can you find those people if you aren't clear on what, beyond hard work, you need them to believe in? If you know your WHY, you can hire people who believe what you believe, which is a much stronger motivator than money. Knowing your WHY is the secret to hiring for "fit."

- **If you're an individual employee,** like Steve, the light-steel salesman who sat next to Peter, knowing your WHY refreshes or renews your passion and connects you to your company's WHY. And should you and that company ever part ways, clearly understanding your own WHY will be an invaluable tool to help choose your next job: a company where you're more likely to "fit," succeed and feel fulfilled.

- **If you belong to a team or division** within an organization, it will likely have its own subculture. In some cases, articulating that team's WHY, the unique contribution the team makes to the organization, can be very powerful. It can help connect those people on the team in a deeper and more meaningful way to the difference the organization makes in the world.

- **If you want to discover the WHY of the entire organization** it will come from one of two sources: The first is from the founder's WHY, which draws from the origin story. If the founder is no longer available, we have a method that engages people in the organization to identify the WHY based on the best elements of the existing culture.

We've divided our approaches to Why Discovery into three chapters that address these categories above. Whether you're a founder, entrepreneur or an employee, you're one person and you will use the *Individual* Why Discovery process, covered in chapter 3. If you are part of a team, group or division within a larger company use the *Tribe* Approach covered in chapters 4 and 5. The Tribe Approach is also the method you should use if you want to discover the WHY of the entire organization and the founder is no longer actively involved.

But before you separate into individuals and tribes, let's jump into the heart of the process, the basic steps *everyone* follows.

Step 1: Gather Stories and Share Them

Each of us has only one WHY. It's not a statement about who we *aspire* to be; it expresses who we *are* when we are at our natural best. If, like Steve the steel salesman, you're already unconsciously living your WHY, then spelling it out for yourself will turn it into an even more powerful tool. And if you're struggling to live your WHY, then finally understanding your purpose, cause or belief can help you change course and realign with a new perspective, a new role or perhaps even a new company to help you find the feeling of fulfillment that may have eluded you thus far.

At its core, the WHY is an origin story. By looking to our past and teasing out the most significant threads—the experiences we've had, the people we've been influenced by, the lives we've touched and the highs and lows we've faced—we can identify patterns. For individuals, our WHY is fully formed by our late teens. To uncover our WHY we must bring together our standout memories— our defining moments—and examine them to find the connections. For tribes, the WHY also comes from the past—either the origin story of how the company was founded or from specific stories shared by other members of the tribe that represent what makes them proud to be a part of the tribe. Either way, discovering your WHY is like panning for gold in the river of the past: the gold is there, lost in the debris of the river, hidden by rushing water. Only when you take the time to pan for the significant moments of the past, retrieving them nugget by nugget, will they turn into treasure.

The more specific the memories, the better. "Our family took a driving vacation every summer"—nope, that's too general to be helpful. "Our family always took driving vacations. One year the car broke down in the desert, and we had to hitchhike to Albuquerque. I was seriously scared,

Leaders are the ones who have the courage to go first and open a path for others to follow.

——

but I remember thinking that I needed to be strong so that my younger sister wouldn't be scared as well, so I made up a game to entertain us"—this is the kind of specific detail you'll need! Rediscovering the details, the feelings, the conversations, the lessons learned will offer clues to who you are and what your WHY is. The more stories you can recover and share, the more data you'll compile. And the more data you can draw on, the more easily you'll begin to see the recurring ideas or themes.

Whether you are an individual or a tribe, press your memory for the stories that have made the biggest difference in your life. Some occasions you recall may be momentous, but many won't be. What's important is the *quality* of the memory, the specific details you remember and the strong emotion you feel as you tell the story to someone else. Because it is very difficult to be objective and see the golden thread that connects our stories, we suggest, whether you follow the individual or the tribe process, that you work with a partner or with a facilitator, respectively.

Are you wondering, "Umm, will this take as long as Freudian therapy?" Relax, there's no couch required. You'll come up with as many specific, impactful memories as you can—at least ten. Once you've got them all down, you'll choose about five or six that made the biggest difference in your life and share them in as much detail as you can.

Step 2: Identify Themes

Did you ever come home from a party and realize that you had a really good time—mostly because you met someone who got you talking about your life growing up or your experiences in your business? Part of the fun that night (besides the joy of hearing yourself talk) may have been that, in hearing the stories, your listener developed an idea of who you are, one that you may have found startling. Instead of being just the middle child, for example, you emerged as the glue that held your siblings together. Instead of being only one of many employees, you turned out to be the new hire who walked in the door and started everyone in a fresh direction by saying, "Why do you guys always do it *that* way?"

Reconnecting with your past to discover your WHY can be fun in that same kind of way. As you pan for your stories and share them, themes will start to emerge, insights about yourself or your team that you may never have expressed before. As the process unfolds, one or two of those nuggets will seem to shine brighter than all the others. They will feel bigger, more important. They will shine so brightly that you'll point to them and say, "That's me— that's who I am," or "That's us—that's our team." These themes become the foundation of your Why Statement.

Step 3: Draft and Refine a Why Statement

With one or two shiny nuggets in hand, you're ready to take a crack at your Why Statement. Try to make yours:

- simple and clear
- actionable
- focused on the effect you'll have on others, and
- expressed in affirmative language that resonates with you.

Eventually, you will put your Why Statement into this format:

TO _____ **SO THAT** _____ .

Yup, that's all it is. Not fifteen paragraphs. Just one sentence. Of course, simple doesn't necessarily mean easy. In one sentence, it's harder to hedge or sidestep or hide behind gobbledygook. One sentence is the absolute lowest common denominator. One sentence is usually more honest. And if you can wrestle your WHY into one sentence, you're much more likely to remember it—and to act on it.

Though we will get into more detail in later chapters, let's break it down a little bit now. The first blank represents the *contribution* you make to the lives of others. The second blank represents the *impact* of your contribution. So, could your Why Statement be, "To finish every project ahead of schedule and under budget, so that I can be promoted and earn enough to save college money for my kids"? No. Even if you see that as the truth right now, your Why Statement will go deeper than that. It is everlasting and must be relevant in both your personal and professional life. It is a statement of your value at work as much as it is the reason your friends love you. We don't have a professional WHY and personal WHY. We are who we are wherever we are. Your contribution is not a product or a service. It's the thing around which everything you do—the decisions you make, the tasks you perform, the products you sell—aligns to bring about the impact you envision.

Let's come at this from another angle by analyzing a real person's Why Statement. Here's how Simon Sinek expresses his WHY: *To inspire people to do the things that inspire them so that, together, we can change our world.* The impact Simon seeks is for each of us to change our world, in big and small ways, for the better. Fantastic! But this goal is too broad and abstract on its own. It's his contribution, what he actually does on Monday morning to make change happen, that gives direction to his desired impact. The contribution part—to inspire others—gives Simon the focus he needs. The books he writes, the talks he gives, the workshops he conducts are WHAT he does—all of them infused with his cause—to inspire people. And the more effectively he inspires others, the more likely every person who is drawn to his work will make a change to our world for the better.

The "**TO** _____ **SO THAT** _____" format works for everyone. It's the simplest way to codify our calling. Whether our WHY is individual or tribal, when we work with a clear WHY in mind, we show up every single day with the feeling that we are part of something bigger than ourselves.

* * *

Many of us are like Steve, the man of steel: even if we're living our WHY, we may find it hard to articulate our contribution and impact in specific words. The Why Discovery process—individual or tribe—is designed to help you put all those gut feelings, all those things that inspire you, into words. For this process you will need:

- **A good partner or facilitator.** Choose someone who'll push you to think beyond the surface, to go out of your comfort zone and uncover the memories and experiences that are the source of your WHY. Very likely, it's your partner or facilitator rather than you who will be able to look down from the perspective of fifty thousand feet and see the themes in your stories.

- **Enough time.** How long is enough? Hard to say. Most likely, more than six minutes and less than six hours.

We will map out all the necessary details in the chapters to come. All we ask, for now, is that you trust the process. It works.

CHAPTER 3

Why Discovery for Individuals

This section is for any individual who wants to learn their personal WHY. Whether you're an entrepreneur, work at a company, are a student or a stay at home parent, the process is the same. If you want to find the WHY of a team or a group, head over to the next chapter, which explains the Tribe Approach.

Like most things, the Why Discovery process is most efficient and effective when you're fully prepared. See the diagram below to get an understanding of the process that you will be going through. Next, we'll walk through these seven steps one by one.

FIND YOUR PARTNER → **GET YOUR PARTNER UP TO SPEED** → **PICK A TIME AND A PLACE** → **GATHER YOUR STORIES**

SHARE YOUR STORIES → **IDENTIFY YOUR THEMES** → **DRAFT YOUR WHY**

Find Your Partner

Remember, to find your WHY you need to pan for gold in the river of your past, recalling stories of your life and career from which your significant themes can emerge. Only you can retrieve those stories from your memory, but when it comes to interpreting them, a second set of eyes and ears—a partner—is invaluable. Listening to your stories, your partner can offer a perspective that is nearly impossible to see for yourself. Finding the *right* partner is an important part of the process. That doesn't mean you must find a trained psychologist or coach, just someone who genuinely wants to help you find your WHY (the "Partner Section" on page 43 will teach them how to do the rest). The role of the partner will be to take notes as you share your stories and to ask questions that will help you find deeper meaning and significance in them. The partner is there to help identify the golden thread, the recurring themes and ideas that are the basis for your WHY.

You don't have to know your partner well, but we recommend that it's someone with whom you feel comfortable sharing personal information and feelings. Though counterintuitive, we don't recommend selecting a partner who knows you *too* well. In our experience, spouses, close relatives and best friends have a hard time being objective. You don't want someone who may be tempted to either tell your stories for you or correct the ones you tell. The best partners will be hearing your stories for the first time. They will be

The best partners are innately curious, which makes them great at listening and great at asking follow-up questions. Someone trying to get to know you a little better will almost always ask more probing, unexpected and thoughtful questions than someone who thinks they already know everything about you.

someone who will listen and take notes as you recall your stories. Again, they are someone who genuinely wants to help you discover your WHY.

Get Your Partner Up to Speed

Once the person you've chosen has accepted your invitation to help, we highly recommend that you start by showing them Simon's talk so they can understand the basic concept of the Golden Circle. To support your partner, we've included that video and the content from the "Partner Section" below online at http://bit.ly/FYWresources. Have your partner read this section before you get started so they can be prepared for their role in the process.

* * *

PARTNER SECTION

Welcome

Thank you for agreeing to help someone discover and begin to articulate their WHY—the purpose, cause or belief that drives them. For us (Peter and David), helping someone find their WHY is one of the most inspiring things we do in our jobs. We love the opportunity to partner with someone and see them light up when they are finally able to put their WHY into clear terms. Even though we've done hundreds of these, it is always inspiring. Now you get to be the partner (we'd be lying if we said we weren't a little jealous). So have fun and enjoy the gift you are about to give someone.

At the end of your time together, the goal is to have a draft version of their Why Statement in hand. This will serve as a filter for the decisions they make so that they can find as much joy and fulfillment in their work and career as possible.

This section is designed to give you the tips and tools you need to support them. Don't worry—you don't need to be a therapist or coach to be a great partner. You just need to have a desire to help your companion find their WHY. We'll be here to guide you step-by-step through the process. In Appendix 2 of this book on page 227, we've also included a summary of all the tips and questions you'll need so that you don't have to refer back to this chapter during the Why Discovery process.

At its core, the WHY is an origin story. Who we are is the sum total of all the experiences we've had growing up—the lessons we learned, the teachers we had and the things we did. In order to help your companion discover their WHY, you'll need to listen to stories from their past. Their WHY represents who they are at their natural best and will be revealed through specific stories and experiences that affected their life and shaped who they are.

Your Role

Your main role is to listen to the stories then ask thoughtful questions that will help them dig deeper to find the underlying meaning of each memory. As you listen, you'll take notes, identifying themes, ideas, words or phrases that recur in the stories; these themes will weave together into a golden thread to define who they are at their natural best.

During this process, it's essential that you put aside your own biases. Don't allow what you know about the person, or even what you think you may know, to cloud your objectivity. What's most important is that you be fully present, meaning you will avoid distractions and stay completely focused on the task at hand. The Why Discovery process is not a therapy session or a mentoring moment; it's not a time for you to offer your opinions and advice or to solve problems. Your job is to be an active listener.

How to Be an Active Listener

Active listening is about hearing more than the words that are said. It's about understanding the meaning, motivation or emotion behind those words. Some of the techniques of active listening are simple: Make eye contact; acknowledge verbally and nonverbally what the other person says (e.g., offer affirmation like, "go on," or nod your head as you understand things); invite them to say more about what happened or how they feel about it. Pay particular attention to *nonverbal* cues. Facial expressions, body language and even long pauses all serve as clues as to how the story makes them feel.

The stories you will hear are some of the most meaningful of their life, and they may evoke strong feelings. Pride, love, fulfillment, fear, belonging, loneliness—all these and more might show up in different ways. Some people get more animated—use their hands more, sit on the edge of their seats, raise their voices—others may get choked up or become soft-spoken and reflective. You won't be able to write down everything they say. However, be sure to take notes of what they are saying when you see a visual or emotional cue—these may be important details as you start to find the common thread later on.

How to Dig Deeper

We often find that people begin their stories with straightforward facts—what happened, when it happened and who was there. It's what we naturally do when we tell stories. While these details are important to set context to what will be shared next, they won't help you get to the WHY, because the WHY is connected to feelings. Sharing feelings is a very important part of the process. The goal is to help them express the feelings and emotions they felt at the time. It's really hard to connect with a feeling when we speak in generalities. We can't stress enough that the stories your companion shares need to be *very specific*. For example, they might at first say, "I used to visit my grandparents every summer during school break. It was a lot of fun." As a partner, you won't get much juice from that. You want the person to connect with a specific summer, a specific event or interaction. If the first pass at the story is unemotional, try digging deeper with something like, "Of all the summers you spent with your grandparents, tell me about the *one* that stands out the most." The goal is that they then actually get specific, which might sound something like, "I remember the summer when I was thirteen. I just had my birthday and I was officially a teenager. I felt really grown-up and wanted to do grown-up things. I remember working in the yard with my grandpa. He let me use the lawn mower and I felt like he trusted me with something important. It gave me a sense of confidence." There's a lot more to explore in that version of the story.

PARTNER TIP

If you notice that your companion starts speaking in generalities or responds with a general story when you ask for something specific, don't let them off the hook just to be nice. It will make it more difficult to find their WHY and much more difficult to tie their themes back to their stories, which is really important. Remember, the WHY is not who we aspire to be, it's who we truly are. The stories are tangible proof of who they truly are.

If they tell you right off the bat how the experience made them feel, don't take what they say at face value; ask clarifying questions. Often, the expression of feelings indicates an underlying and significant lesson or a particular relationship that embodies who they truly are today. If emotions are the proverbial smoke, the underlying meaning is the fire. And where there is smoke, there is fire.

It's your job to ask follow-up questions until you uncover the reason this specific story is significant. Here are a few questions that may come in handy (you can find a summary of all the tips and questions in Appendix 2 on page 227).

- How did that make you feel?

- What is it about this experience that you absolutely loved?

- You've probably felt this same feeling before. What is it about this story that makes it special? (E.g., if they say they "felt proud," you can ask them what about this pride was different from other times they felt it.)

- How did this experience affect you and who you've become?

- What was the lesson from that experience that you still carry with you today?

- Of all the stories you could have shared with me, what makes this specific one so special that you chose to tell it?

- If someone else features prominently in the story, ask them how that person made a difference in their lives or what they love or admire about that person.

You'll know you're getting somewhere when they begin talking less about what happened and more about how they felt about what happened. It might sound something like, "It just really filled me up to be a part of that," or "It was pretty disappointing to know that I let my parents down." Statements like these are where you want to start digging. For example, what do they mean by "filled up" or "disappointed"? You may assume you know, but their definition may be different from yours. So ask a question that will elicit more specifics, such as:

- Tell me what you meant when you said, "It really filled me up."

- You've probably felt disappointed before. Describe how this particular feeling of disappointment was so different that it still comes to mind all these years later.

You may hear stories that are not particularly warm or happy. That's normal. There is lots to learn about someone from their positive *and* negative experiences. Your job as the partner is to help "see" the lessons or even the silver linings in those difficult moments too. For example, we did a Why Discovery with someone who, when asked about a happy experience from her childhood replied that she had a horrible childhood. She then went on to recount stories of an extremely physically abusive father. What we heard, however, was that in every story, she always mentioned how she protected her sister from her father. She never realized that pattern existed. As soon as we pointed out the silver lining, the positive glimmer in such a dark experience, she immediately started crying. She is who she is today because she's learned to protect those who could not protect themselves. Happy memories and sad memories, tales of opportunity and hardship, all offer a chance to learn about who someone is and how they became who they are. All roads lead to WHY.

The better you capture the themes of how they felt, the easier it will be to put together the Why Statement that feels really authentic to them.

In addition to the recurring themes that you'll listen for in each story, there are two other main components to look for: contribution and impact. These are the building blocks of the final Why Statement—the contribution the person makes to the lives of others and the impact of that contribution over time. We write it in this format:

TO _____ **SO THAT** _____ .

The contribution is the first blank and the impact is the second blank. For example, Simon Sinek, the author of *Start with Why*, expresses his own WHY in these words: *To inspire people to do the things that inspire them so that, together, we can change our world.* Simon's contribution is what he actively does for others (seeking to inspire them) and the impact is what happens when that contribution is made (a lot of people working together to change our world).

With that in mind, do what you can to find out what your companion is giving someone else or receiving in each story (the contribution) and what difference it may have made to them or others (the impact). You'll begin to see a pattern that will help you understand the contribution and impact of their WHY. There is almost always some sort of emotional cue, verbal or nonverbal, when they touch on one or both of these themes.

Some Tips for Asking Great Questions:

- **Ask open-ended questions.** The best questions are those that can't be answered with a yes or no. They require the person to give more information. Often in our workshops we hear people ask questions like "That made you angry, didn't it?" This question is unhelpful for three reasons: it can be answered with yes or no, it assumes you know how the person will respond and it "leads the witness." They may agree with you, though they may have answered differently if left to answer an open-ended question without your help. Remember, this process relies on getting to the heart of who they are, not who you think they are. Instead of leading the witness, try something like, "Help me understand how that made you feel."

- **Avoid questions that start with "why."** This may sound counterintuitive, since you are doing a Why Discovery. But there's a problem with questions that start with "why." Ironically, they are actually harder to answer. "Why does that story matter to you?" for example, triggers the part of our brain that is not responsible for language. It's easier to answer a question that starts with "what." For example, "What is it about that story that really matters to you?" It's basically the same question but framed in a way that is easier for someone to answer. It answers the "why" question by allowing the person to talk more specifically about the components of the story that were meaningful. Try both; you'll see what we mean in practice.

- **Sit in silence.** If you ask a question and feel they are struggling to answer, let them struggle. Though your inclination may be to help fill in the silence, don't. Resist the temptation to fill the silence with another question or a suggested answer. Instead, just wait. Emotions are difficult to articulate and it may take the person a little time to formulate the right words. Sometimes silence is the best tool you have to get them to tell you more. Master it.

How to Take Notes
(PS: This is the last section—you're almost done!)

Surprisingly enough, the format you use to jot down your notes can be really helpful when it comes time to help your companion tie

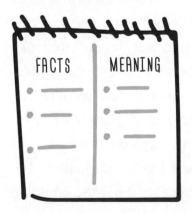

everything together. You can take notes however you'd like, of course, but we've found this format especially useful; maybe you will too.

Draw a vertical line from the top of your notes page to the bottom (an example has been included for you in the appendix). On the left side of the line jot down the factual details of the story (e.g., college graduation). On the right side focus on their feelings, emotions or interpretations of the meaning of the story (e.g., cared that he made his grandfather proud). On the right side you can also write down any words, phrases, verbal or nonverbal cues that come up more than once. Separating your notes in this way makes it easier to review them at the end and identify the elements that are most important to the Why Discovery process (hint: all the essential stuff will be in the right-hand column).

As you take notes on multiple stories, you'll begin to notice which themes, words, phrases or ideas recur most often. Underline, circle, highlight or put a check mark next to each of those words or phrases. This can help you quickly identify the themes that will lead to the WHY later on. Also, for each story write "contribution" and/or "impact" in the right-hand column to remind you not to move on to the next story until you are clear on what they gave or received (the contribution) and what effect it had on them or others (the impact).

We've given you a lot of details that we hope will help you be the best partner possible. Remember, this really matters to your companion and they asked *you* to help them. That's an honor. What matters most is that you show up with a genuine curiosity as well as a desire to help the person you're working with. Who knows—maybe, when it's all over, you'll be inspired to look for your own WHY

* * *

Pick a Time and a Place

How about the Starbucks that's equidistant between your office and your partner's? Definitely not. You're about to have an intimate conversation. Noise and distraction will only make it more difficult, even if there is a Smoked Butterscotch Frappuccino to be had. Plus, you'll be exposing a lot of personal information—why do it in a spot where all those people pretending to work on their screenplays can overhear you? Choose a place where you can concentrate and where you feel free to share personal stories out loud.

While a phone call or video conference with your partner can work, we strongly suggest that you meet in person. That way it is easier for your partner to pick up on body language (not just facial expressions) and other visual cues that are only available when you're in the same room. If you do have to work remotely, settle down in a quiet, distraction-free location and encourage your partner to do the same.

And set aside enough time—at least three hours. Yes, that's a big commitment, but there is no shortcut to discovering your WHY. Think of it as working out. The more time you put into it, the more you get out of it. It's not the kind of thing you can race through.

As you learned in chapter 2, there are three steps to discovering your WHY (tell stories, identify themes, draft the Why Statement). It works best when you complete all three steps in one sitting. If you stop after two or three stories, for example, and try to resume a few days later, you'll have to get into storytelling mode all over again. In fact, we highly recommend that you work through all three steps without interruption (except for a few breaks and leg stretches, of course). Identifying themes right after telling your stories is much easier than trying to come back to the task later. Similarly, drafting your Why Statement will be easier when the recurring themes and patterns that emerged from the stories are fresh in your minds.

Turn off your phones, remove any distractions and enjoy the process.

Gather Your Stories

Before meeting with your partner, you need to do a little prep work. Your WHY is born from your past experiences; it is the sum total of the lessons you learned, the experiences you had and the values you adopted while growing up. You're looking for stories that bring to light who you are at your natural best. As you recall stories that fit the bill, jot down notes on each so you can quickly recall them when you sit down with your partner. Here are a few guidelines for gathering the type of stories that will lead you to your WHY.

- Think of specific experiences and people in your life that have really shaped who you are today. You may choose an event that was obviously important, such as the day you came up with the idea for your company, or an event that's less obvious, like a defining moment you had with your old boss. If the event meant something to you, helped you become who you are, taught you something or made you proud, write it down. As you think of the people who have been the most influential in your life, try to recall specifics about what they said or did that made such a difference to you.

- Since your WHY comes from your past, which is the period from your birth until yesterday, you can draw your stories from any time in between those markers. The memories may come from school, home, work or any other area of your life. You may recall times or events that you would gladly revisit. Or you may retrieve memories of painful episodes that you would never want to relive. What both kinds of experiences have in common is that, good or bad, they helped make you who you are.

Our struggles are the short-term steps we must take on our way to long-term success.

——

The goal of the story-gathering exercise is to end up with at least five stories that you consider the most impactful of your life. The more stories you have, the easier it will be for your partner to detect the patterns and themes that will lead to your WHY. Remember that each story must be about a specific time, place or moment. The more specific you are, the more you'll feel an emotional connection to that memory. And it's this emotional connection that will lead to your WHY.

Write down your stories as they come to you. As you begin, keep in mind that all roads will eventually lead to WHY. So don't overthink this process. You may list your stories chronologically or at random. Don't worry about writing down all the details. A simple line or two for each is sufficient. The goal is simply to have a starting point for sharing the stories with your partner. When you share your stories with your partner, you can include all the particulars and explore any additional memories that may pop up.

Here are a couple of story-gathering methods we've found helpful; you can use one, both or neither.

Method 1: Peaks and Valleys

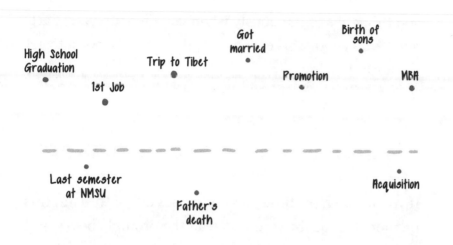

Draw a horizontal line across the middle of a piece of paper. Stories you put above the line are those you consider happy memories: moments you'd enthusiastically relive. Stories below the line are events that you wouldn't necessarily want to relive but that impacted your life and shaped who you are today. Write a few words to encapsulate each story as you fill out the chart. The higher you plot the stories above the line, the more fulfilling and positive they were. The lower you plot the stories below the line, the more challenging or difficult they were. You'll probably end up with stories at various levels.

When it comes time to choose the stories you'll tell your partner, choose the highest of the highs and the lowest of the lows. These are the stories that carry the most emotion and therefore the ones that will most clearly lead to your

WHY. You probably won't share all the stories you've noted on the page; in fact, you may share other stories that you think of spontaneously when you are with your partner. It's all good. This exercise is just a starting point to get the juices flowing.

Method 2: The Memory Prompt

If you have a hard time picking stories out of thin air, this method may be for you. Just read the prompts below and see what memories they spark. Don't worry about writing down all the details. Just write a line or two on a piece of paper to jog your memory when it comes time to share with your partner.

- Who in your life has helped make you the person you are today (coach, mentor, teacher, family member)? Write down a specific time when they exemplified what you admire most about them, whether they were interacting with you or with someone else. How did hearing their words or watching their actions make you feel? Who else helped shape who you are today? Repeat as many times as you like.

- Think of a day at work when, as you headed home, you might have said to yourself, "I would have done that for free." What happened that day to make you say that?

- Think of your worst day at work—the kind of day you hope never to go through again. What happened?

- What is the earliest, *specific*, happy childhood memory that comes to your mind?

- At school, what was an experience you loved?

- What has been a pivotal moment in your life, one when you realized nothing would ever be the same?

- What happened that changed the way you think about the world and your role in it?

- What was a time when you gave of yourself to help someone else, after which you felt unbelievably good—like you had done something that mattered?

- What have you accomplished that you're really proud of? (Be sure to make a mental note of who else was involved. For example, who helped you, who cheered you on, who was waiting for you at the finish line?)

Once you have your chart or list of stories in hand, you're ready to share them with your partner. Just a word of caution. Again, don't overanalyze your selection of stories before you meet with your partner. One of the main reasons you work with a partner is to have someone who can find meaning you can't see and offer objective, open-minded insight. If you come to the storytelling part of your Why Discovery with preconceived ideas about how your memories fit together, you risk telling them in a way that proves your theory. Relax and let your partner identify the themes. You are the storyteller. Your partner is the interpreter.

SHARING TIP

One little trick that can help the process is to circle the three most impactful stories you have and tell those to your partner first. By focusing on the most impactful ones, you'll avoid the temptation to tell stories that just seem to tie together.

It's the Little Things That Count

David conducted a Why Discovery workshop with someone named Todd. The following is a story Todd told David; it's the kind of story you might tell. Many people think they have to tell big stories of major events to find their WHY. What's nice about this example is that although it seems like a relatively small story in the scheme of things, David was able to use this story to assist with finding the golden thread that helped Todd articulate his WHY.

Prior to this story, Todd shared other details about his life. How he went to college on a full basketball scholarship but ended up losing it due to drug and alcohol addiction. He had aspired to make it to the NBA, so this more than ended his college career—it also shattered his dreams and his self-identity. He was working at a bar, still battling drug addiction and alcoholism and contemplating suicide, at the time this story took place:

Todd: I had gotten off work and was driving up a winding road on my way home one Saturday morning. I passed a little girl selling lemonade outside her house. On any other day, I would have driven past. For some reason, on this day, I had an inexplicable urge to turn around and give her all of my change.

I pulled my car up to her lemonade stand and asked how much a cup of lemonade was. "Twenty-five cents," she told me. So I said I would take one. She walked back to the stand to get me a cup of lemonade, and while she was doing that, I scooped out all the quarters I had in the cup holder in my car. They had been piling up from all the tips I get at work. I probably had close to forty dollars in there. The girl handed me the cup of lemonade, and I put a fistful of quarters into her little palms. And then another scoop. And then another. Each time I watched her eyes light up. She turned and ran into the house full of excitement.

I drove away feeling good, as you might expect. But then something happened that I didn't expect. I suddenly became overwhelmed with emotion. I started crying uncontrollably. I was crying so much I had to pull my car over. It was amazing.

David: Wow. That sounds intense. I'm sure you've done things in the past that made you cry. Of all the stories you could have shared with me, what specifically is it about this one that made you choose to share it?

Todd: It was the first time in my life that I felt that I had done something for someone else. It was the first time in my life I hadn't put myself first. This was a huge wake-up call for me. It lit my soul on fire and for the first time I felt like I mattered. I wanted so much to help others feel like they mattered too. I wanted to help others feel they could do and be more. From that moment on, I wanted to share with the world what I had felt.

By the end of the Why Discovery, David found a thread of service that ran through many of Todd's most significant stories. As he did with the little girl selling lemonade, Todd's WHY is *to ignite people's imaginations about what's possible so that they can find the motivation to do more with their lives*. What's magical about Todd's WHY is that is exactly what happened to him. His imagination was ignited, and he was motivated to do more with his life.

Share Your Stories
(This Is Where Your Partner Comes In)

Your preparation is complete. Now it's time to sit down with your partner and find your WHY. It can feel uncomfortable to share this much about yourself, but you don't have to abandon your comfort zone entirely—we just want you to push the boundaries a bit. If some stories are just too personal to reveal, then don't tell them. But for the ones you do choose to share, know that the more you open up, the easier it will be for your partner to see the significant patterns. Share only the stories you feel right about sharing. But when you do share, allow yourself to be vulnerable enough for the process to work. You may surprise yourself with how open you can be as the process unfolds.

Specificity is key to the process. We can't emphasize this enough. When you made your list or chart of stories, we told you not to worry about the details. Now it's time to dig in. Tell your stories in as much detail as you can. Keep in mind that by "details" we don't mean the temperature on a given day or the outfit you were wearing (unless those were particularly significant details to the story). While this kind of information can provide context, the information we're really interested in goes far beneath the surface. Since feelings are at the heart of your WHY, it is vital that you connect viscerally to your memories and the emotions you experienced at the time. Specific stories will allow you to do this is in a way that general statements won't. The following are some examples:

General Statement: We used to go to my grandparents' house every year for Christmas. It felt so good to be surrounded by loving family.

Specific Story: We used to go to my grandparents' house every year for Christmas. The year that really sticks out in my mind is when I was nine years old. That was the last Christmas my grandfather was alive. He was a powerful force in my life, and I'm not sure I realized how powerful until he was gone. I had a great relationship with him, but only now do I see how he rubbed off on me. He was a crazy, eccentric character who marched to the beat of his own drum. People called him strange or odd, but he always seemed perfectly normal to me. I remember sitting with him on the couch—just him and me. I was also an odd kid, people called me weirdo at school. But with him I felt safe. With him I felt proud to be me, proud to be different. Thinking he was the coolest person ever gave me the confidence to be my weird self. If he was odd and that amazing—well heck, I better get comfortable being who I am if I want to have the same impact on my kids or grandkids one day.

General Statement: When I was a kid I really loved gymnastics. I practiced every day for four hours. It was challenging, but I got a lot out of it.

Specific Story: When I was a kid, I really loved gymnastics. Practices were long and intense. I remember one day my team and I were working on some tumbling with my most demanding coach. This guy was really tough to please. He was so hard on me. I never felt good enough for this guy. Sometimes I felt he had it out for me, that he was harder on me than the others. No matter how hard I worked, it was never enough. Tumbling, especially aerial work like twisting flips, wasn't my strong suit. But I kept at it because I was determined to prove to this guy that I was good enough. And then it happened. I remember it like it was yesterday. I remember after one run I took, my coach kneeled down next to me and said to the rest of the team, "That's how it should be done!" I never felt prouder. I realized at that point that he was harder on me not because he didn't like me, but because he believed in me. He pushed me because he knew I had the work ethic and he knew I had it in me. Instead of telling me, he wanted me to learn that I had it in me. I realized at that moment that discipline and hard work, which were ingrained in me at home, were really important. I think that's when I really learned about grit. I still get chills thinking about that day.

General Statement: I love my job. I've traveled to a lot of great places and some not-so-glamorous ones too. What's pretty consistent, though, is that I'm always meeting interesting and inspiring people. The pay isn't bad either!

Specific Story: I love my job. I get to go to some wonderful places, but even when my destination isn't glamorous, some of the most inspiring things happen. I remember a specific time I went to a city that I wasn't looking forward to visiting. It was a small, rural community and I thought, "Well, win some, lose some." At the event I attended there, I met a football coach from a nearby university. This guy was amazing. As we talked, he shared the most wonderful story about how he does things differently. He runs his football team as a human development and leadership program. Most coaches care only about winning and losing. This coach cares about the growth of his players first. If they win, he doesn't let it get to their heads. And if they lose, he uses it as a learning opportunity. Here's the best part: it's having a huge impact on his players. Not only are they performing better as a team, but most of them are doing better in school and even having more success with personal relationships, like with their families, all thanks to their football coach. It was one of the most inspiring stories I've ever heard. And I'm not even a sports fan!

The general versions of these stories say more or less the same thing as the specific versions. But notice the depth of emotion expressed in the more specific versions. Digging deeper brings back how you really felt

As you share your specific stories, your partner should take notes about the situations and circumstances you describe and also the feelings they evoke. At the risk of beating a dead horse, these notes will be instrumental in identifying the material *and* emotional links between your stories. The goal is not simply for you to describe things you did but to uncover who you are.

Spend as much time as you need to tell each of your stories fully and to venture beyond your original list. As you share, you may remember experiences that you had forgotten. Tell those stories too. Remember, all roads lead to WHY. There are no hard and fast rules to the stories you tell. Whether they are from your preparation or spontaneous memories, any story of significance, can help solidify themes or introduce new elements for consideration. The more stories you can share with your partner, the more data you will be able to cull from to find the golden thread. And the clearer the golden thread, the more accurate your Why Statement will be.

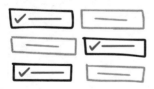

Identify Your Themes

The next step in your Why Discovery is to identify themes: the recurring ideas, words, phrases and feelings that emerged from your stories. Your partner should take the lead during this part of the process. Remember, your partner has an objectivity that you don't have simply because you're too close to see the patterns. While you're busy describing trees, your partner has a better view of the forest emerging.

We see this all the time among people who want to learn their WHY. They think they can play both roles—storyteller and partner. They try to analyze their own stories and identify the themes themselves. We have yet to meet a single person, however, who has successfully done it. (But we've met plenty who claimed they did it, then they showed us a Why Statement that was about their business or their family or some goal they wanted to reach. When pressed, their statements or their "passion" for their statements fell apart.) Even when Simon developed many of these techniques to discover his WHY, he asked someone to hear his stories and help find the golden thread for him.

Again, your partner is focused on listening and recording and has the benefit of objectivity. They are often hearing the stories for the first time, free of complicating factors such as personal history, insecurities or ego. That's the reason the themes tend to be more obvious to them.

Just as there are no wrong stories, there are no wrong themes. If something comes up more than once, write it down. There's no limit to the number of themes your stories may yield. You may end up with eight, ten, fifteen or more. That's okay. The first step for you and your partner is getting all the themes down on paper.

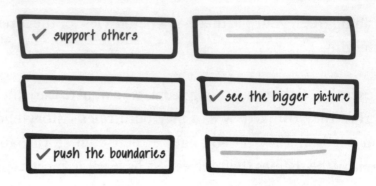

With your themes all in one place, take a couple of moments to look them over. In some cases, the theme will be in every story. However, your partner should be able to tie each theme back to at least two of the stories you told. Remember, an idea becomes a theme because it reoccurs in at least two seemingly unconnected stories.

With all the themes listed, circle one or two that seem bigger than the rest—those that jump off the page. The ones that inspire you or seem to define you and what you care about most. Is there one you love more than the others? Ask your partner to weigh in on which of the themes seem more important, based on the stories you've told. Together, choose one theme that feels like your unique contribution and one theme that captures the impact. Now you're ready to draft your Why Statement.

Wait a second, you may be thinking. If those two themes are the only ones that will be used in the Why Statement, then why does my partner have to bother writing down all the other themes from my stories? And what if I really love themes that didn't end up in my Why Statement—do I have to just throw them away? Don't worry! There's an important reason your partner writes down all of your themes, and, no, they don't get thrown away. As we'll see in a later chapter, those themes will become your HOWs.

Draft Your WHY

Once you've identified your overarching themes, it's time to turn them into a draft of your Why Statement. As we noted in the previous chapter, we recommend that your first draft follow this format:

To _____ ← Contribution

so that _____ .
← Impact

This is the easiest way to ensure that your statement is simple, actionable and focused on how you positively affect other people.

With your overarching themes in mind and this format in front of you, take a few minutes and write a first draft of your Why Statement. Your partner, working separately, should do the same. The value in writing independently at first is that your partner may articulate your WHY differently than you do. Be it the perfect word or catchy turn of phrase, we find that having two slightly different takes on a Why Statement is actually very helpful. It's the same principle as taking a friend shopping with you. They might pick out a shirt that you wouldn't have looked at twice. But then you try it on and it's the greatest shirt ever.

Spend about five minutes both working on your own statements. Only five minutes because there is little value in overthinking at this stage. Then rejoin your partner and share your respective drafts. After considering both Why Statements, you may choose to go with one or the other or to combine them.

Remember, the goal of this draft is not perfection. The goal is to get it in the ballpark, to come up with something that *feels* right. The actual words can, and likely will, change as you continue to spend time with your WHY, reflect on it and, most important, put it into action. This is what the final step is all about.

Refine Your Why Statement

After you have a draft, the final stage of the Why Discovery process is testing and refining your Why Statement. There are a few ways to do this. One fun way to validate your Why Statement, or to get ideas for how to tweak it, is to do what we call the Friends Exercise. For this exercise, make a list of your closest friends—the people who are always there for you, the ones you can call at 2:00 A.M. if you need them and know they will pick up the phone. The ones who, if they called you at 2:00 A.M., you'd be there for them too. Then follow the instructions below. You can also download the Friends Exercise as a free PDF at http://bit.ly/FYWresources.

Friends Exercise

The exercise works best if done in person, one friend at a time. Be sure to give your friend some context about the process you've gone through, and tell them that you're asking them to help you on your journey. Keep your WHY to yourself for now. You don't want to influence your friend's upcoming responses.

First, ask them, "Why are you friends with me?" Don't be surprised if your pal looks at you as if you've grown three heads. It's not a question most friends ask each other, and it's harder to answer than we think. Friendships are rooted in feelings and, as we know, feelings are difficult to put into words. For this exercise to work, you have to keep going even if both of you are a little uncomfortable.

Ironically, asking a question that starts with "why" doesn't actually get us to the WHY. That's because the question "why" is an emotional question, and it tends to elicit vague or reactive answers. In contrast, asking a "what" question elicits a more thoughtful and exact answer. Now ask the same question again, this time framed with "what": "What is it about me that made you choose to be friends with me?" This time your buddy may say something like, "I don't know. I care about you. I can trust you. We're into the same stuff. And we just get along really well!" That's a logical answer, but of course, those are the basic elements of almost any friendship. Continue to play the devil's advocate, always framing your "why" questions with "what." For example, if you want to ask "why . . . ," instead ask "what is it about . . ." Follow up with something like, "Great, you've just defined what it means to be a friend! But *what* is it about *me* in particular?"

Your friend will probably stammer and struggle for a minute and maybe even come up with more attributes of any friend. As this goes on, you'll find it more and more tempting to let them off the hook, but keep at it. "Yeah, but what *specifically* is it about *me*?" Continue to push them beyond the rational answers.

There are two ways you can tell that you're getting where you want to go in this conversation. The first is when your friend goes quiet and starts staring at the floor or ceiling, seemingly at a total loss for words. What's actually happening is they are connecting with their feelings for you and struggling to put them into words. If you attempt to fill the silence by throwing out another question or comment, you'll interrupt this very important process. Instead, let your friend sit in that silence and work through it. Let's say you're doing this with one of your friends. At some point, your friend will move on from generalities, such as "We have the same sense of humor," to something specific, such as "You really make me laugh . . . which is fun, but which also makes me realize that we see the world the same way. When I tell you what my boss said last week, and you make a joke about it, I not only laugh, but I also feel reassured that my boss is the crazy one, not me."

And that brings up the second thing to watch for, which is a distinct shift in your friend's focus. At some point, they will stop describing you and seemingly start describing themselves. In the example above, when your friend says, "I feel reassured that my boss is the crazy one," they are not talking about your personality but about how you make them feel and the difference you make to them. In other words, your friend is articulating your unique contribution to their life. And you've gone deep enough when you have an emotional response to whatever they say. You may get goosebumps or get choked up. That's because they have put into words the true value you have in their life. They have stated your WHY in their own words, and because the WHY exists in the part of the brain that controls emotions and not language, you have an emotional response. This is an important turning point. It's a wonderful way to see how you've been living your WHY without even realizing it.

Chances are that the themes and patterns that emerge from the Friends Exercise will be similar to, if not exactly like, those you and your partner uncovered during the Why Discovery process. But maybe your friend used a word or phrase in talking about you that you like better. If it feels right, go ahead and incorporate those words into your Why Statement. On the flip side, if the Friends Exercise brought different themes to light, that's something to consider too. Do any of those themes sit better with you than the ones you identified during the Why Discovery? If so, maybe you and your partner need to do a little more digging.

In addition to the Friends Exercise, it can also be helpful to just let your Why Statement sit for a few days. Think of it as a cake. When you pull a cake out of the oven, you can't cut a slice and eat it right away. It's too hot and it will fall apart. The cake needs time to cool and set. Your WHY is the same. Give it some time to cool and set before you start to use it.

Often the first draft of a Why Statement sounds a bit generic. While you are sitting with your WHY, try to unpack the words to find language that is more authentic to you, that more completely captures your feelings. We sometimes play a little game with people and ask them if they like the words in their Why Statement enough to have them tattooed on their body. If the answer is no, then you haven't found the words you "love" and relate to yet. You really want to *love* the words, especially the words of your contribution.

As you revise your Why Statement, refer back to your stories. This will help ensure that any changes you make won't water down the accuracy of the statement. In the end, the goal of refining your Why Statement isn't to make it *sound* better; it's to make it *feel* better.

How much time does it take to hone your Why Statement? We really can't say because it's different for everyone. Finding the perfect words for your WHY could take weeks or months. You may go through one iteration or a dozen. That's proved true even for members of the Start With Why team.

Take David, for example. David's Why Statement used to read:

To propel positive change so that people can live a more fulfilled life.

This statement was in the ballpark, but the phrase "fulfilled life" didn't feel exactly right to David. It was too broad and, it seemed to him, somewhat clichéd. So he spent some time digging deeper. He had to answer the questions, "When I 'propel positive change,' what am I actually doing? And while I'm at it, what does 'a fulfilled life' mean?" He lived with his Why Statement and practiced saying it and implementing it—all the time making little tweaks until this got to something that felt even more like himself than the previous version.

The answer resulted in a revision of his original Why Statement:

To propel people forward so that they can make their mark on the world.

What David realized when he thought more deeply about his word choice was that, for him, to propel people to live a fulfilled life meant helping them be a little better than they were the day before so they can have a greater positive impact on others—and that specific definition of "fulfillment" is spelled out clearly in the second version. That's why David's current Why Statement is stronger than the first: because it is both more precise and more personal.

Refining your WHY might make it more powerful for you, as it did for David. But it won't make it more valid or actionable. The words don't need to be perfect in order for us to begin to put our statement into practice. As former Secretary of State Colin Powell said, "I can make a decision with 30 percent of the information, anything more than 80 percent is too much." In fact, as you live with your WHY it will become easier to find the perfect words, because you'll be more conscious of your goal and how you're trying to reach it. So take some time to sit with your Why Statement, but don't sit for too long. The reason to find your WHY is so that you can act on it.

We envision a world where everyone knows their WHY. Well, we know that reading a book is not the only way, or even the ideal way for some, to discover their WHY. As we are dedicated to having a Golden Circle on every desk, we've created multiple ways to find your WHY. Our team conducts live events and workshops and we have resources available online. Learn more and find tools to inspire at www.StartWithWhy.com.

CHAPTER 4

Why Discovery for Groups

Part 1: The Tribe Approach

In this chapter, we will help you prepare for the Tribe Approach to the Why Discovery process; in chapter 5, we'll lead you through the specific steps to conduct the workshop. The Tribe Approach is intended for any group that wants to articulate their common purpose, cause of belief—to put into words what an organization's culture is like when it's operating at its natural best, even if the organization is not currently performing at that level. We define a "tribe" as *any group of people who come together around a common set of values and beliefs*. A tribe can be an entire organization or a small team. Often, where you sit within the organization determines who you view as your tribe. If you are the CEO of an organization, everyone who works within the organization is your tribe. If you are the director of a division, the people who work in your division are the members of your tribe. If you are the leader or member of a team, the team is your tribe. If your organization's structure isn't so clearly defined, rely on what feels right. It's possible that a team member may fit into more than one tribe. The bottom line is a tribe is the place where you feel you belong.

At this point you might be thinking this is sounding like one of those mathematical word problems you did in grade school. The purpose of doing a Tribe Why Discovery is to simplify things, not to add complexity. We use a concept called "Nested WHYs" to help explain the idea. Nested WHYs should only be used if they genuinely deepen people's relationship to the WHY of the organization and the part they play in it. If the overarching WHY is enough to inspire people across the organization, stick with that.

Nested WHYs: Defining a Part of the Whole

An organization has a WHY. And within an organization are teams—subcultures that exist within the larger group. Each of these parts within the whole will have its own WHY. We call that a Nested WHY—the purpose, cause or belief that defines a subgroup within the larger organization. Then within each of those teams are people who also have their own unique WHY—their individual WHY. The goal is for each individual to work for a company in which they fit the culture, share the values, believe in the vision *and* work on a team in which they feel like they are valued and valuable.

A Nested WHY always *serves* the company's overarching WHY; it never *competes* with it.

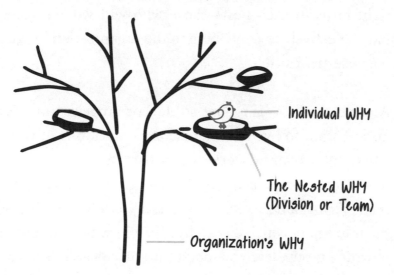

Individual WHY

The Nested WHY (Division or Team)

Organization's WHY

The reason to articulate a Nested WHY is the same reason an organization would want to articulate the big umbrella WHY—because it gives people a sense of identity and belonging. It allows teams and groups to identify with the people they work with every day. It helps them understand their unique contribution as a distinct group to the larger vision.

Think of the organization like a tree. Its roots and trunk represent its origin and foundation. In that tree are branches—those branches are the divisions and departments of the organization. And on those branches sit nests—those nests are the subcultures or teams in the tree. And within each nest is a family of birds who belong together. The goal for us as individuals is to know our WHY so that we can more easily find the right tree *and* the right nest. The goal for an organization is to know its WHY in order to attract the right birds. And the goal for each team within the company is to make sure that they have the right birds in each nest—those who will work together most effectively to contribute to the organization's higher purpose and cause.

America has a WHY—but so do Los Angeles and New York. I want to live in America; the question is in which city should I live and work? It is possible for someone to be in the right company but in the wrong nest. This can hurt their performance, morale and self-confidence. Helping them to know which city to live in, which nest to join, or in which group, team or subculture they best fit is part of the jigsaw puzzle of building a thriving organization. Some companies have it down to a science how to attract and hire the best fits for the company. However, the art is knowing where in the company they will work at their natural best. Simply hiring a good fit for the company is only part of the work. Knowing where in the company that person will work at their natural best and feel like they are contributing in a way that inspires them is also important. In fact, it can actually be more important.

We have worked with companies that have a very fuzzy sense of WHY. Leadership is not that interested in "soft" stuff like purpose, cause or belief, so they ignore it. However, the leaders of some of the subgroups in the company who do believe in this stuff took the time to articulate their group's Nested WHY.

As one would expect, those groups tend to have the highest morale, are the most productive and innovative, have the best retention rates and over time are some of the highest performing groups in the company.

* * *

Simon Sinek, the founder of our company, has a WHY: *to inspire people to do the things that inspire them so that, together, we can change our world.* His WHY is also our company's WHY, and we all believe in and embrace that WHY. In fact, that WHY is the basis of our shared vision—

to build a world in which the vast majority of people wake up every single morning inspired to go to work, feel safe when they're there and return home fulfilled by the work that they do. However, inside our company we have teams that work together on a regular basis. And over time, subcultures have formed. The group in which we, Peter and David, work has a Nested WHY: to shine a light on what's possible so that together we can transform our world. This is our group's unique contribution to the company's higher purpose. Simon's books, talks and workshops are very inspirational. This book, you will find, is more focused on shining light on how to actually do the things he talks about. This is not an accident. This is our nested purpose—showing people the way is why we come to work in the morning. It's how we contribute to our company's purpose.

Let's take it a step further. Our whole team shares that Nested WHY. However, we are also individuals in that nest. Each of us makes our own unique contribution to our collective WHY. So within the team, each of us has an individual WHY that's all our own.

Everything Peter does is designed *to enable people to be extraordinary so that they can do extraordinary things*. David gets out of bed every morning *to propel people forward so that they can make their mark on the world*. We both complement our company's WHY. Where Simon lights a spark, our team shines a light and fans the flames to show people exactly how to breathe life into our vision. Every individual in our company knows their individual WHY, they know the Nested WHY for their team and they know the shared vision we are all working to advance.

* * *

Here are a few points to consider before setting up your tribe's workshop if you're discovering the WHY of the entire organization:

- If the founder is still part of the organization, doing a personal Why Discovery with the founder can be a great place to start. Founding their organization was just one of the things they did to bring their WHY to life. Articulating their personal WHY will give context and will be in the ballpark of the WHY of the greater organization. We've conducted a few tests in which we've facilitated both a personal Why Discovery with the founder and then used the Tribe Approach with a larger group. When the culture is strong, it's eerie how similar the results are.

- If the founder of a company is no longer alive or isn't available for consultation, the Tribe Approach is the best way for an organization to find or rediscover its WHY.

If there is more than one founder, choose the visionary. Often companies are founded in pairs. There is a visionary and a builder or several builders. See chapter 12 in *Start with Why* to learn more.

Here are some specific situations in which a subgroup might consider doing a Tribe Why Discovery to articulate their Nested WHY:

- When a unit or division feels it would inspire their tribe to discover their Nested WHY to better relate to and complement a clearly articulated company WHY. Remember, a Nested WHY is always subordinate to the organization's WHY. If a subgroup tries to come up with its Nested WHY in a vacuum without considering the reason their group needs to exist within the larger company, it may end up working at cross-purposes with the rest of the company. This can cause confusion. Nested WHYs should always complement the WHY that sits above them.

- The exception to the above statement is when a unit, division or middle manager within an organization wants to find the WHY of their subgroup because those at the top of the hierarchy are not interested in articulating the company's overall WHY. If the larger organization really has lost its way, is operating without a clear sense of WHY and the senior leadership has no intention of going through a Why Discovery, any leader of a team or member of a team can become the leader they wish they had. Though not ideal, it is a solution that we've seen inspire other groups to follow, and, eventually, the tail wags the dog and the larger corporation comes along.

An organization that's highly dysfunctional—perhaps as the result of a merger, acquisition or some other development—is *not* operating at its natural best. It likely has no unified sense of purpose, which results in a group of individuals or silos trying to advance their own interests. When dealing with this sort of situation, we recommend taking the Tribe Approach with a smaller group within the organization, one that has managed to maintain strong leadership and a healthy culture. Helping this group articulate its WHY can be a first step toward "wagging the dog."

If you'd like to learn more about "wagging the dog," Simon Sinek covers the topic in chapter 7 of his book *Start with Why.*

The great thing about a Why Discovery for a subgroup within an organization (i.e., a Nested WHY) is that it can influence the whole organization to want to find its WHY. When a single division starts to think, act and communicate based on its WHY, good things happen: performance tends to improve, innovation tends to rise, employee turnover tends to decline. Senior management notices these developments. Employees in other divisions notice, as well, because the people in the WHY group tend to enjoy coming to work more than they did before. After we did a Tribe Why Discovery for one small division, the phone started ringing with calls from employees in other parts of the company, asking if there were any positions available. In that way, the tail can wag the dog, meaning, a small group of inspired and engaged employees can have a positive impact on the entire organization.

However, there may be times when the culture is so weak that no suitable subgroup exists for a Tribe Why Discovery. In these cases, the only thing that can right the ship is strong, visionary leadership. A strong leader, even if that person isn't the founder, can give a WHY-less company a sense of purpose.

Supplying a WHY where none existed before is very different from changing an existing WHY. A company's WHY is made up of cultural norms, common values and strong relationships, and a new leader can't simply come in and change those things. A leader *should* supply a new WHY when the company's original purpose has been completely destroyed by years of misuse and abuse. The best scenario in this situation is for the leader to complete an Individual Why Discovery. They can then lead the company based on that WHY, and those inspired by it will follow.

Though it's rare, we have come across a few organizations that are completely dysfunctional and broken, where fear, mistrust, paranoia and self-interest run rampant. In a case like this, a Why Discovery turns into a vent session in which people simply spill out their frustrations, prejudices and complaints in ways that move nothing forward. What we'd advise an organization like this to do is to call in a third-party facilitator or consultant who can help the organization's leaders identify the underlying cause of the many problems. Only after this deeper analysis is com-

pleted will clear space be created for an effective Why Discovery. Without this prework, a Why Discovery is almost
certain to fail—and once that happens, it is extremely difficult to succeed on a second try. It's much easier to set
yourself up for success from the start by dealing with any
deep-seated problems first.

Stories Embody the Why

Peter did an organizational or Tribe Why Discovery for a company called La Marzocco. Before the workshop Peter talked with a few members of the leadership team to learn a bit about the company's history since the original founders were no longer there. In 1927, in Florence, Italy, Giuseppe and Bruno Bambi founded La Marzocco to build espresso machines by hand. Over the decades that followed, the company has employed a dedicated team of craftsmen who have been a model of innovation in the industry. Its machines are still built by hand, each signed by its maker, and are bought by coffee aficionados and specialist coffeehouses worldwide.

Peter used the Tribe Approach in the workshop and heard many stories from employees trying to articulate the pride they feel for La Marzocco as an organization. He heard someone say, "We're the Rolls-Royce of coffee makers and have developed a cult following to rival Harley-Davidson." They talked about the workers' incredible pride in their product, touting how they lavish as much attention on the unseen parts as on the highly polished stainless-steel exteriors. They told specific stories about their customers being equally enthusiastic. The team from the customization department talked about the machines they painted or decorated to each individual customer's taste. A story was shared of a customer who even had a tattoo of the company's logo on their arm. It was clear to Peter that around the world, La Marzocco stands for something meaningful to customers and employees alike. Putting this feeling into words was the tricky bit.

Peter pushed the workshop attendees to dig deeper. He said, "La Marzocco makes coffee machines. That's the company's WHAT, but it's not the whole story. La Marzocco isn't about pressing a button on a dispenser and watching a plastic cup drop down, then waiting for a computer program to fill it. I think we're getting closer when we talk about baristas explaining the choice of beans and different roasts. And I feel a surge of energy when we talk about machine owners—individuals or businesses—who invest as much passion and care in using the machine as the workers did in fabricating it. There is something more, let's keep going."

An employee raised his hand to share a story he felt really embodied what La Marzocco stands for. He talked about the coffee-related events the company sponsors around topics such as leadership, community and sustainability. He told a specific story about an event at a Milan hotel where the company hosted a photography exhibit that featured a coffee-growing community in Tanzania. He said La Marzocco didn't just invite its customers and partners, it also welcomed competitors. A DJ was flown in from a Seattle radio station because his mission is to foster global community via music. And, of course, there was coffee. He said the event was powerful because there were so many opportunities for people to talk and connect.

On the heels of that story, another teammate said, "La Marzocco is about sitting down and engaging with others over a cup of coffee. It's about bringing people together to savor life."

Following that statement was a series of audible validations. A few people threw their hands in the air, someone else clapped.

By the end of the workshop, everything just described about La Marzocco made sense when they read the company's Why Statement: to cultivate relationships so that the lives of others are enriched. Yes, La Marzocco makes coffee machines. That's WHAT they do. But why they do it is more human. They are obsessed with bringing people together; that is their cause, and coffee machines happen to be the business they have found to help them advance it.

* * *

Now that we've clearly identified who your tribe is, it's time to prepare you for your tribe's Why Discovery workshop. Before we get into the details, here's a road map to help you visualize the steps that lie ahead.

**FIND
YOUR FACILITATOR**   **PREPARE FOR
YOUR SESSION**   **INVITE
PARTICIPANTS**

We recommend that you prepare by taking the following steps.

Find Your Facilitator

The Tribe Approach requires a facilitator. The ideal person for this role is someone trusted by the organization who has a desire to serve, a strong natural curiosity and an ability to ask probing questions. While a professional facilitator can bring confidence and experience to the job, it's not necessary for the process to be successful. If you're not a seasoned facilitator, or if one is not available, don't worry! We wrote this book to help you take on the job.

The facilitator must be objective, so think of someone who has a little distance and perspective—for example, an outsider, someone who wasn't present at the founding of the company and isn't one of its long-standing executives. This ensures that the facilitator won't accidentally bring preconceptions or biases to the process. In other words, sometimes knowing less is more. Working with an objective facilitator also means they can *run* the process rather than be *part* of it.

That said, we realize it may not be possible or practical to bring in someone from the outside. If this is the case, you can choose one of your colleagues to act as facilitator or choose to do it yourself. As long as the foundation of the process is understood: that a WHY is discovered, not created, and that the Why Discovery process is not aspirational. Nor is it a branding or marketing exercise. Approaching the process that way would completely undermine everything that makes a true WHY so compelling. The WHY is about who we are, not what we'd like the company to become someday.

Whomever you choose, the facilitator will lead a group in a workshop setting. This requires its own unique set of skills: the abilities to manage time and logistics, to listen actively and to draw connections from various contributors. The facilitator also needs to create a "safe" environment in which people, regardless of rank, position or personality, feel comfortable sharing their thoughts and stories.

This list of capabilities and attributes may seem daunting, but, in truth, anyone who loves to learn and is comfortable working with a group should be able to lead a Tribe Why Discovery. Of course, the more practiced they are, the better. Above all, they need to have a strong sense of curiosity and to be excited about the idea of leading the session. In the end, if you *feel* comfortable with the person, it's likely they will be able to create the environment that will promote a great Why Discovery. Think of it this way: There are lots of equally well-qualified doctors out there, but given a choice, we will select one over another. Why? Because we like how that doctor makes us *feel*. Apply the same thinking when you select your facilitator, and you'll be in a good position to move forward.

The remainder of this chapter and the entirety of the next chapter are addressed to the facilitator of the Tribe Why Discovery. Based on what you've read so far, if you feel that you aren't the right fit for that role, choose someone who is and ask them to read the next section and the other chapters it references. If you do plan to fill the facilitator role, keep reading. The rest of this chapter and chapter 5 are for the facilitator to prepare to run the Why Discovery process for tribes.

Prepare for Your Session

It's an honor to have been asked to take on the role of facilitating a Why Discovery workshop. We recommend a few things to ensure you're fully prepared for the workshop. In addition to reading this chapter, you should also look at chapter 3, which explains the Individual Why Discovery process. You won't follow the steps in that chapter for this specific workshop, but the more familiar you are with the foundations of the discovery process, the more equipped you will be to lead the tribe through it. If you are willing and time permits, before undertaking the Tribe Why Discovery, we suggest you practice by taking a few individuals—colleagues, friends or acquaintances—through the individual process.

Before you get to the Why Discovery process itself in chapter 5, there are some important tasks that you as the facilitator—or someone assisting you from within the organization—need to perform:

- Invite participants
- Schedule enough time
- Find the right setting
- Set up the room in advance

Invite Participants

The Tribe Approach requires at least ten to fifteen participants but can accommodate as many as thirty. If you go above that number, you need a very experienced facilitator, someone who is skilled at keeping large groups on task; otherwise, the process can become long, unwieldy and messy. So if you're new (or even newish) at facilitating this process, limit your group to a maximum of thirty.

Why no fewer than ten? It's the job of the participants to generate stories that are a diverse representation of the organization as a whole. Remember, we're attempting to capture a universal statement that, in its nature, will resonate with all members of the organization. We're trying to articulate the WHY; that is, if we revisit the tree analogy, we're trying to establish the foundation (the roots and the tree trunk) upon which all branches and nests sit. If we end up with too many birds on one branch or on one side of the tree, it's likely that we will accidentally articulate the WHY of a subculture or of a single branch or nest. The end result will be that when they hear it, every bird in the tree may not feel they belong. No matter the size of your organization, make sure to have a cross section of all of its parts.

The exception to the "minimum of ten" rule is an organization with fewer than ten people. In this case, those ten people represent the entire tree. Everyone in the organization is involved in multiple aspects of the business, and the group usually has exactly what they need to articulate the organization's WHY.

We find that Tribe Why Discovery sessions are most successful when the majority of participants share two characteristics: zeal for their jobs and reasonably long tenure in the company. Participants who have worked at the company for a long time will have more stories and experiences to call upon. And if they've been around long enough, they will have seen the company go through good times and hard times, when it was operating at its natural best and when it faced its biggest challenges.

Even though they may have fewer stories to share, you may choose to invite a few new employees to participate. Hearing the stories, learning some of the folklore and getting to know their colleagues in a more personal way often catalyzes their sense of belonging and boosts their pride in the new job. They have a special insight to offer: since they recently joined the organization, the reason they chose to do so is presumably still fresh in their minds. New teammates can also share objective insights that may be less obvious to someone who has been working at the organization for years.

The other key quality to look for in participants is passion for the company. You want as many zealots in the room as possible. These aren't necessarily the top performers, though some of them may be. The zealots are the ones who "get it." The ones who regularly sacrifice their time and energy to make the organization better. The ones who care most about the company. The zealots represent the company at its best.

If for political or other reasons you also need to invite some nonzealots, that's okay. The process is objective and these few "misfits" will likely not bias the results. In fact, sometimes they fit in better than expected because the workshop helps them share the reasons they love the organization. But even if it doesn't, as long as they are in the minority, the process will work as designed.

Finally, if you are doing a Tribe Why Discovery for an entire organization (as opposed to a subgroup), we recommend that you choose participants who represent a cross section of the company—individuals of different ranks from a variety of departments or divisions. This will ensure that the WHY you uncover is truly the organization's WHY and not a WHY nested within it.

In our experience, the ideal number of participants for a Tribe Why Discovery is twenty to thirty. A group this size can generally draft a Why Statement within four hours. Figuring out just how many people you'll need in the workshop to get the best results requires trusting your gut.

A team is not a group of people who work together.

A team is a group of people who trust each other.

_____

Sometimes an organization prefers that all the partici-pants be drawn from the ranks of senior leaders. This ap-proach can work as long as the leaders meet the basic requirements: tenure and zeal. The majority of partici-pants, regardless of rank, should be people with substan-tial experience at the company who love working there and care about the people and the culture. A Why Discov-ery with senior staff must also represent a good cross sec-tion of job functions. The process will not work otherwise. If you have an imbalance from engineering, for example, you are more likely to end up finding the WHY of the engineering department, not the WHY of the whole com-pany. Balance is critical.

Schedule Enough Time

A Tribe Why Discovery takes at least four hours, but orga-nizations may try to compress the session into a shorter timeframe. Resist! Having the full four hours is crucial. Having five hours is even better. It's like cooking a turkey. You can try to speed things up by increasing the oven tem-perature, but even if the bird looks brown on the outside, it's not going to be cooked all the way through. To feel good about their Why Statement and take ownership of it, the participants have to go through the full intellectual and emotional journey. They have to bring the WHY to life through the stories they share. We have done many discoveries where we could have identified an organization's WHY in under an hour—but we wouldn't have brought the group along with us, emotionally. People need to make the discovery on their own, and, for a group, that takes time. It won't matter how wonderful the Why Statement sounds if no one in the organization feels ownership of it or is inspired to bring it to life in their work.

Find the Right Setting

Why Discovery requires a kind of thinking that can be quite different from the kind most people do every day. A space that inspires creativity, fosters privacy and minimizes distractions is ideal. The environment you choose—whether it's within the company's offices or at an outside location—should promote these things in the following ways:

Choose a space large enough that participants can break into small groups. Participants will sometimes work on their own, sometimes in groups. So in addition to being well-ventilated and well-lit, the space needs to be large enough and flexible enough to allow people to move around and/or to rearrange the tables and chairs. You also need room for a snacks-and-drinks table, which will help keep everyone focused for the full session.

Choose a space where the group won't be interrupted. If a room has noisy neighbors, contains the only copy machine employees need to use or is located on a busy corridor that people constantly traverse on their way to somewhere else, it's not a good choice.

Set Up the Room in Advance

The dynamic in the room from the moment the workshop begins really matters, so we will discuss the room's set-up in detail. Set up the room in advance to avoid using valuable workshop time rearranging the room according to our directions below. Doing this will ensure that participants experience the intended atmosphere from the moment they walk in.

- *Arrange the furniture:* Though there's no one right way to do this, we prefer the horseshoe. If possible, move tables back to the walls and arrange the chairs in the shape of a horseshoe. The circle helps generate open discussion by eliminating any sense of hierarchy.

- *Choose a way for groups to capture their ideas:* We generally provide flip charts on easels for each group. (For group size and how to determine the number of groups, see chapter 5.) Large sheets of paper or whiteboards can do the trick as well. Remember to provide pens or markers, preferably in several colors, and make sure they work.

- *Set up your flip charts:* Position three additional flip charts on easels at the front of the room. Those are for you to use. (We prefer to use flip charts, rather than whiteboards, because they allow us to quickly refer back to something written down earlier in the session.)

- *Set up the projector and screen:* If you choose to use a slide deck or computer, make sure that the required technology is in place and functioning properly and that participants' view of the screen is unimpeded.

Here's a sketch to help you picture the ideal room set-up:

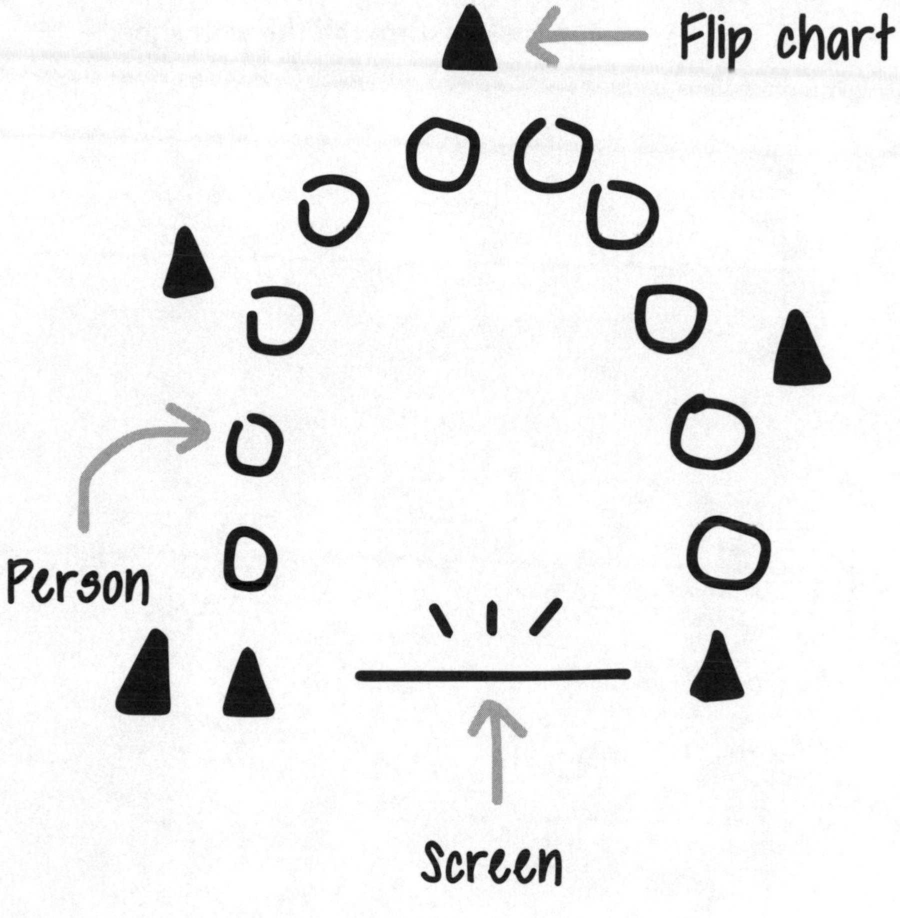
Flip chart
Person
Screen

Here ends your logistical preparation for running the Tribe Why Discovery.

We're ready to move on to the next chapter, where we walk you, step-by-step, through the workshop.

CHAPTER 5

Why Discovery for Groups

Part 2: Talking to the Tribe

FACILITATOR SECTION

You read in chapter 4 that there were two main tasks for the facilitator: to *prepare* for a Tribe Why Discovery and then to *lead the workshop*. We walked through the preparatory steps in chapter 4. Now we'll talk about everything you need to do in order to guide your group through the session. If you're new to this experience, we recommend that you closely adhere to the guide. The less you have to worry about the process itself, the more you can put into listening, questioning, analyzing and engaging. If, on the other hand, you are a practiced facilitator, you will likely put your own twist on these instructions and come up with some ideas of your own to make your group's discovery even more successful.

The Why Discovery workshop has three main actions:

- Set the context
- Run the Why Discovery Process
- Draft a Why Statement

Now we'll explain these steps in detail and suggest an approximate time frame for each.

**SET
THE CONTEXT**

**RUN THE WHY
DISCOVERY PROCESS**

**DRAFT
A WHY STATEMENT**

Set the Context

(🕐 **45–60 MINUTES**)

A great way to begin a Tribe Why Discovery is to bring in a senior leader, someone who is respected within the com-

pany or group and is already 100 percent on board with the concept of WHY, to explain the reason the session is happening and discuss its significance. That person can also acknowledge how much time the participants are investing in the process. When we know our sacrifice or allocation of time is appreciated, we give it more willingly. The idea is to reassure participants that they have *permission* to focus fully on the session. This may seem like an obvious point, but individuals often hold back when they feel they should be doing some other work that is "more important" to the company. We want participants to know that *this* is important work and they have permission to fully participate.

Having an enthusiastic senior leader introduce the session will also serve to "let you in" as the facilitator. This is especially important if your relationship with the company or group is new. By opening up the session and giving you the floor, the senior leader effectively announces that the company trusts you to guide the group through the Why Discovery process and asks the participants to give you their undivided attention and cooperation.

After you have been introduced and the floor is yours, we recommend you begin by sharing a short WHY story. Sharing a personal WHY experience can go a long way toward forging a bond with your audience. If you're struggling to find a story you're comfortable sharing, you can use one of the stories we tell in this book (such as Steve, the "man of steel" in the introduction or La Marzocco in chapter 4) or any story you find appealing from Simon Sinek's book *Start with Why*.

(His descriptions of Apple [Inc.] and Southwest Airlines as companies with powerful WHYs are very clear and compelling.)

Whatever story you choose to tell, it should illuminate what's possible when a group of people are united in service to a higher purpose. It should also illustrate how a common WHY can inspire loyalty in a tribe. The story will function both as a real-life link to the reason for the session—to find the organization's WHY—and as evidence of the reward to be won by those who stay present and engage in the process.

By this point, you will have spoken for about ten minutes, depending on the length of your opening story. That's plenty for now. It's time to give the group the opportunity to talk. Invite everyone to pair up with the person beside them (if you have an uneven number, there can also be trios) and come up with a response to this prompt:

- If you think back to the time when you joined the organization, what inspired you most? What inspires you to keep coming back?

FACILITATOR TIP
Participants often sit next to people they already know and are comfortable with. It is valuable to mix up the room to have people engage in conversation with someone they don't know as well.

Give the pairs four to six minutes to share their thoughts with each other. Tell them at the get-go that each person in the pair gets two to three minutes of speaking time. To ensure that all voices are heard during this time, gently remind the group, when the time is halfway up, that the idea is for *both* partners to share.

This simple exercise generates good conversation, which is just what you want. The primary purpose is for everyone to participate actively, rather than sit back and watch the workshop happen around them. And because telling stories often prompts emotional responses, this exercise is also a perfect opportunity to prepare the group for what will follow. While there's no need to have everyone present their story to the full group, you might invite one or two people to share the inspiring story that their partner told them. Although the participants probably won't realize it yet, these stories are likely connected to the organization's underlying WHY.

Now that the group is engaged, it's time to lay the foundations for the rest of the session by explaining the crucial concept of the Golden Circle.

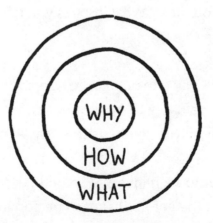

We introduced the Golden Circle in chapter 1. If, as facilitator, you have only read the Tribe Why Discovery chapters, you may find it helpful to read chapter 1 now.

Once you're ready to communicate the Golden Circle to your group, an easy way to begin is to show them Simon's TED talk video (http://bit.ly/GoldenCircleTalk). Alternatively, you can review the concept with them yourself—free slides and notes are available at http://bit.ly/FYWresources.

Your aim is to make sure everyone understands these Golden Circle fundamentals:

- WHATs are products, services and job functions we perform. HOWs are values, guiding principles and actions that make us stand out. The WHY defines what the organization stands for—it is the collective purpose, cause or belief.

- It's human nature to go from what's easiest to understand to what's hardest to understand. In terms of the Golden Circle, most of us think, act and communicate from the outside in (WHAT–HOW–WHY). Those with the capacity to inspire do it differently. They think, act and communicate from the inside out (WHY–HOW–WHAT).

- The WHAT corresponds to the neo-cortex, the "newest" part of our brain, which is responsible for rational, analytical thought and language.

- The WHY corresponds to the limbic brain, which is responsible for our feelings, such as trust and loyalty. This part of the brain drives all human behavior and decision making but has no capacity for language. This is how we are hardwired; it's biology, not psychology.

- People don't buy *what* you do, they buy *why* you do it.

- When a company has a strong WHY, it inspires trust and loyalty in its customers, clients, employees and supporters, all of whom will cheer you on in your cause.

At some point early in the workshop—before, during or after you introduce the Golden Circle and the concept of WHY—it's entirely possible that you will be challenged by one or more members of the group. We certainly have been. People may say, "This all sounds a little bit fluffy," or "This is not the reality of business." Remember, you are trying to get people to think in a new way, so meet them where they are. Respond as best you can—we've offered some guidance on how we answer common questions in the "Frequently Asked Questions" appendix at the end of this book (page 213). The most important thing is to ask these members of the group to trust the process and keep an open mind. Again, the idea is not to convince someone of the value or validity of having a WHY; the idea is to create an environment in which they may come to those conclusions themselves and can contribute to finding their group's WHY.

Next, offer participants a broad overview of what they should expect from the rest of the day, starting with a general time frame, including breaks. Explain that the remainder of the session will have two main parts, each with its own goal:

- *Story Sharing:* The goal is to collect specific stories that reveal both the contribution the organization makes to the lives of others and the impact of that contribution over time.

- *Drafting the Why Statement:* The goal is to take the themes that emerge from the participants' stories and use them to write the first draft of the tribe's Why Statement: its purpose, cause or belief.

Limbic brain: See chapter 4 in *Start with Why* for more on this topic.

Emphasize the word "draft" in the final goal. Let the group know that the aim is to write a Why Statement that is 75–80 percent complete. This is due to the WHY coming from our limbic brain. Explain that they don't need it to be perfect; they need it to be actionable. You'll come back to the reason for this later.

Run the Why Discovery Process

(🕐 2–2.5 HOURS)

Sharing personal stories and identifying their themes are critical pieces of the Why Discovery process for individuals and groups alike.

In the Tribe Approach, we achieve this through what we call the Three Conversations.

The Three Conversations

An early Apple slogan once proclaimed, "Simplicity is the ultimate sophistication." These conversations are simple, but that doesn't mean they're easy. The tough part is that participants are forced to find language to express how they feel. For a few people, this will be easy enough, but most participants find that having these conversations takes considerable energy.

There will likely be times during this process when everything seems messy, when you don't seem to be getting the responses you need

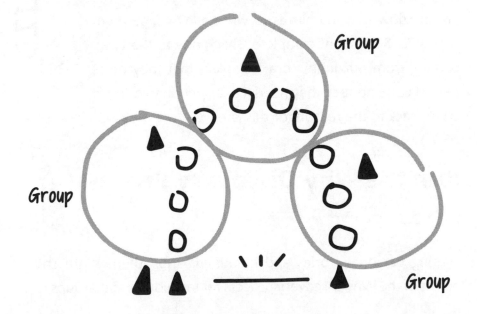

or to be moving closer to WHY. Trust the process. Remember, this exercise is more about the *feeling* that is generated in the room than the exact words that come out of the conversation.

The first step in the exercise is to divide the group into three teams of roughly the same size. The easiest way to do this is to split the room between left, right and rear (see diagram on the previous page). Ideally each team will be composed of individuals of varying roles, positions, genders and length of time at the organization. If you don't think the left–right–rear approach will yield enough diversity within teams, you can be more intentional in your assignments. This is not the NFL draft. We're not suggesting you line everyone up and study their CVs before you assign them to a team. Just use your basic awareness of the demographics in the room and you'll do fine. The more diverse the experiences represented on each team, the more dynamic and engaged the conversations. And, as discussed earlier, we want people to think differently in this group than they usually do—working with new and unfamiliar people tends to make that happen.

Once the teams are established, each group should gather around a flip chart and easel. Encourage teams to get up and stand around their respective flip charts, rather than move their chairs closer. Standing releases energy and makes the process more interactive.

You will now present the teams with a starting point for each of the three conversations. We recommend that you project each prompt onto a screen as you introduce it; that way you can be sure that everyone in the room can easily see it and refer back to it as necessary. For each prompt, you will give some direction on how to engage in the conversation and then allow time for team members to discuss among themselves.

FACILITATOR TIP

It's best if you don't share any of the prompts with the group in advance. You want participants to share the first thoughts that come to mind. If you give them the prompts beforehand, they'll probably overthink things, which could negatively impact the process.

CONVERSATION 1: THE HUMAN DIFFERENCE

(⏱ 20 MINUTES)

. . . .

Tell specific stories of when you have felt most proud to work for this organization.

. . . .

(This isn't about money or other metrics; it's about what you have given, not what you've received. Tell stories that capture what this organization stands for at its best.)

If a movement is to
have an impact it must
belong to those who join it
not just those who lead it.

_____

FACILITATOR TIP
You can choose to replace the word "organization" with "team," "group," "division" or whatever noun is appropriate. But the phrasing should not be otherwise modified. We've written it this way for good reason. We're not looking for the organization's financial accomplishments here. We're looking for something more human, something more meaningful that elicits an emotion.

Before the teams start to discuss their responses to conversation 1, provide the following guidelines:

- Each team's task is to write down, on its flip chart, a sentence or phrase that will help team members recall their stories later.

- Generalizations are no good. You want stories about *specific* people and *specific* moments. The more specific, the better. "I'm proud of the quality of the work we do" is too general. "I was so proud the night I met a woman at a holiday party and she told me that her child's life had been saved by a cancer drug we developed. I don't even work in that division, but it reminded me of the importance of our work" is better because it's more specific and emotional.

- The outcome described in the stories can be big or small, affecting thousands of people or just one person. The important thing is for the story to cause a visceral, emotional response in the person telling it.

- Teams should come up with as many *quality* stories as they can (at least three) within the allotted time.

FACILITATOR TIP

In some groups, senior people dominate a discussion to the extent that equally valid ideas from others don't get heard. If you feel this is beginning to happen, step in and encourage those who haven't spoken yet to contribute their stories.

Conversation 1 is not the sort of thing people are used to hearing. So you'll probably see some puzzled faces. That's okay. Let the group sit with the prompt for a bit. But once teams start to talk, be prepared to help them stay on track. To give an idea of the sort of output you are looking for, here are some stories the La Marzocco team shared when Peter did this exercise with them and an example of how the team might take notes on their flip chart.

- "In 2009, we held our first Out of the Box event. This is where we brought together our partners from around the world—suppliers, roasters, baristas and other lovers of coffee. Over two extraordinary days, we shared thoughts and ideas and really just celebrated life. It was meant to be a one-off, but the feedback we received was so wonderful it's now a biennial event." (On the flip chart: Out of Box Event=celebrated life.)

- "We love bringing people together. Recently, we sponsored an exhibition showing photographs of people who work on a coffee farm in Tanzania. The photos are immensely evocative and really help us feel connected to the origin of the beans and those who produce them. While the theme is coffee, it goes deeper than that; it's about relationship. Some of the proceeds from the exhibition are being used to support the coffee-farm community." (On the flip chart: Tanzania Photo Exhibition—supporting the farm community and building relationships.)

- "We work with a coffee roaster in Mexico, in a region where not many people have access to formal higher education. Our company has a policy of hiring people based on who they are and the passion they have—not on the certificates they hold. This has been a huge success, with many of those hired rising to senior positions." (On the flip chart: Our Hiring Policy—passion versus certificates.)

- "In an airport, I met someone who has owned the same La Marzocco machine for twenty years, and it still works perfectly. I felt so proud that in a disposable world my company stands for excellence, tradition and value." (On the flip chart: Loyal Customer—excellence, tradition and value.)

Reporting Out: Sharing the Stories
(🕐 25–35 MINUTES)

When time is up, each team will report to the rest of the room, sharing its top two or three stories. By "top" we mean those that resonated most with the team members—the stories that caused the greatest visceral response. People will express how they feel in different ways; they'll get goose bumps, animated, excited or even choked up. Emotional reactions are cues for you, as the facilitator, to dig deeper. Ask the storyteller to say more about their feelings or what it was about that particular story that evoked such an intense reaction. Returning to the examples from La Marzocco, here are a couple of probing questions Peter could have asked to heighten the storyteller's emotional connection to the organization's contribution:

- "Say more about the feedback from the first Out of the Box event. What did people enjoy so much? What were some of their comments?"

- "Tell us about the photographs in the exhibition. Did any in particular stand out for you? What was it about those particular photos? What has changed in the lives of those coffee workers? Can you give us a specific example?"

FACILITATOR TIP
The route to WHY is through WHAT. Instead of asking questions that start with "why"—for example, "**Why** did you like those particular photos?"—ask "**What** was it about those particular photos?" People find it easier to answer questions starting with "what" or "how" rather than "why."

We usually allow twenty minutes for sharing stories, but be prepared to let the conversation go longer. This is an immensely valuable part of the process because it's rare that they get together in a group to think beyond the numbers and reflect on what their organization contributes to others. This is the reason you should allow four to five hours for a Tribe Why Discovery—you want to have the flexibility to let the conversation flow. Once all teams have shared their stories, they'll be ready to tackle the second conversation.

CONVERSATION 2: WHAT'S YOUR CONTRIBUTION?

(⏱ 10 MINUTES)

In each of your stories, what was the specific contribution your organization made to the lives of others?

Express it in the form of a basic verb/action phrase:
"to (verb)."

Working in the same three teams, participants should start a fresh flip-chart page and write down the verbs or action phrases that capture the essence of the contributions implied or expressed in the stories about what made them proud. Before the teams begin, clarify the goals of this particular exercise by explaining that:

- Verbs are important because our ultimate aim is to discover a WHY that is actionable, not merely descriptive.

- The verbs/action phrases should not be aspirational. This is about what people in the company *have* done, not what they *hope* to do or be.

- The verbs/action phrases must be directly linked to one or more of the stories the team identified earlier. This link is vital. If it is missing, there is the risk that the task will turn into the type of branding or marketing exercise in which words are chosen because they "sound good." Tell the group they must support their action phrase with a story that clearly demonstrates the connection.

FACILITATOR TIP

A good way to keep people on the right track is to have them try to complete the phrase "*In this story we showed up and we _____ed.*" Tell them the blank must be filled by a verb. (For example, see page 181—"More Tribe Examples.")

- Since the teams will consider stories that occurred in the past, the action phrases will likely be in the past tense. However, we want to use the infinitive form of the verb—"*to _____*"—since that will help us later in the process.

- Each team should come up with at least ten verbs/action phrases and no more than will fill a single flip-chart sheet.

You will generally find that people are able to engage in and complete this conversation quite quickly. Ten minutes is usually ample time.

Here are some of the verbs and action phrases that appeared on La Marzocco's list when Peter did the company's Why Discovery:

to engage	to inspire
to enrich	to trust
to build	to enjoy life
to connect	to love
to bring together	

 ## Reporting Out: Gathering the Themes
(⏱ 10–15 MINUTES)

Once each team has completed its list of verbs and action phrases, it's time for them to share with the larger group. Ask a member from each team to call out their words. Now it's time to use your flip chart. Write each verb or phrase on one of the flip charts at the front of the room. Even better, have a volunteer do the writing so you can concentrate on regulating the pace at which words are called out. When you move on to the next team, do not start another flip-chart page. Capture all the verbs and action phrases offered up by the various teams on a *single page.* That page will be very important later on.

Make sure teams call out all their verbs or action phrases, even if some are the same as or similar to what another team has already said. If a team does supply a verb or phrase that has already been written on the flip chart, don't write it down a second time. Instead, add an asterisk to the verb or phrase every time it is repeated. Sometimes two teams will come up with phrases that are similar but not identical. For example, one might say, "To foster creativity," and another might say, "To promote freedom of thought." The fact that they are thinking along the same lines is a good thing. It means that their stories illustrate a *consistent theme* within the organization. If you can, have the two teams agree on a consolidated version as you go along. Record that version on the flip chart and mark it with an asterisk. In all, this reporting process usually takes ten minutes.

You should now have a single flip-chart page at the front of the room showing all the verbs and action phrases that have been called out, with asterisks marking how often a specific idea has been repeated. If you stand back and look at the list, you should begin to see a number of themes. On La Marzocco's flip chart, for example, a theme emerged around "to engage," "to connect" and "to bring together." There's perhaps another theme captured by "to enrich" and "to enjoy life." The exact nature of these themes will be brought home by the stories that are behind them.

Break
(🕐 15 MINUTES)

Managing the energy in the room by scheduling breaks is important. Equally, we want to avoid having breaks that last too long, because this can cause the group to lose momentum. Every group and session will be different and your job as facilitator is to recognize the appropriate times to call a break. We generally have one break after conversation 2. It's up to you as the facilitator to decide what's best. Setting up the room properly and having refreshments and amenities on hand will help breaks run on time.

CONVERSATION 3: WHAT'S YOUR IMPACT?

(🕐 15 MINUTES)

After the break, have everyone return to their small teams to work on conversation 3. There's usually quite a buzz in the room by this point. People will have started to connect to the work they do in a different, more meaningful way. This third conversation is designed to deepen that connection.

What did the contributions of your organization allow others to go on to *do* or *be*?

(Think about how people's lives were different after they interacted with your organization when at your best.)

As people consider their responses, instruct them to refer back to their stories from conversation 1. Again, the goal here is for each team to build on its earlier stories by focusing on the *impact* of the contributions they described. Urge them to think about the specific people in their stories. What were those individuals able to *do* or *become* as a result of the organization's actions? Remind the group that this is not about numbers or other metrics. What you are looking for is the larger impact, the real *human* impact. You'll know that they have begun to hit on this when their responses become visceral and emotional. Using a blank flip-chart page, they should record a sentence or phrase that captures the impact of those contributions.

FACILITATOR TIP

Sometimes when people get into this conversation they tend to diminish the impact they and their organization have had on the lives of others. They may even talk about their competition and how those companies do the same thing. If this happens, bring them back to their stories. The competition may have a similar WHAT, but it doesn't have the same WHY stories. The Tribe Approach is not about the competition. It's about determining what this organization believes in and WHY it exists. Before we can stand *out*, we must first get clear on what we stand *for*.

To get an idea of what this looks like in practice, check out some of the things the La Marzocco group said about its organization's impact. We've reprinted their stories from conversation 1 (in italics) along with their answers to conversation 3 so you can clearly see the connections between the two. (These written answers are more detailed than what we'd expect to see on teams' flip charts. We've expanded the group's answers a bit to help them make more sense as you read them now, out of their original context):

- *"In 2009, we held our first Out of the Box event. This is where we brought together our partners from around the world—suppliers, roasters, baristas and other lovers of coffee. Over two extraordinary days, we shared thoughts and ideas and really just celebrated life. It was meant to be a one-off, but the feedback we received was so wonderful it's now a biennial event.* One of the relationships that grew from this event was between Andrija, a barista based in Serbia, and Catalina, a coffee shop owner in Barcelona. Her coffee shop had become a meeting place for entrepreneurs to develop new ideas and businesses. This inspired Andrija to create a similar shop in Serbia, and it subsequently became the catalyst for several new businesses, making a significant difference to the local community. Without the Out of the Box event, it's likely that none of this would have happened."

- *"We love bringing people together. Recently, we sponsored an exhibition showing photographs of people who work on a coffee farm in Tanzania. The photos are immensely evocative and really help us feel connected to the origin of the beans and those who produce them. While the theme is coffee, it goes deeper than that; it's about relationship. Some of the proceeds from the exhibition are being used to support the coffee-farm community.* The money raised makes a real difference to the quality of life of Elisa-beth, one of the women in the photographs, and her fellow coffee pickers. But the exhibition's effect goes beyond that: It has also helped raise awareness of and appreciation for the work the pick-ers do. As a result, they feel considerably more valued and fulfilled."

- *"We work with a coffee roaster in Mexico, in a region where not many people have access to formal higher education. Our com-pany has a policy of hiring people based on who they are and the passion they have—not on the certificates they hold. This has been a huge success with many of those hired rising to senior positions.* Emilio, for instance, has become head roaster, a position that has allowed him to pull his family out of poverty. The initial opportu-nity transformed Emilio's life and has also inspired those around him, so they now see possibility where before they did not."

Give the teams a total of fifteen to twenty minutes to discuss con-versation 3. At this point, your role as facilitator is to stand back; you should intervene only when a team needs help to stay on track. You may notice that this conversation, in particular, elicits intensely emo-tional responses from participants. We've seen some of the toughest businessmen become teary-eyed when given the chance to pause and think about the difference they've made, through their work, at a fundamentally human level. Even people who seem cool and un-emotional during the workshop may approach you afterward to confess privately how moved they were. When people experience these kinds of feelings, whether they realize it or not, their connection to the organization's WHY is being reinforced.

Reporting Out: Capturing the Impact
(🕐 20–30 MINUTES)

As with the other conversations, after the discussion wraps, teams will share their responses to conversation 3 with the larger group. Now it is time for you to take a more active role. You will need to be fully engaged, listening and summarizing. Allow twenty to thirty minutes for the remainder of the exercise.

To begin, have two fresh flip charts at the front of the room—you're going to need the space. Invite each team to share their output from conversation 3. Your job is to listen for the single line in each response that encapsulates the *impact* of the action, the difference it made in the lives of others. Make note of these on your two flip charts so everyone can see them. Just as with conversation 2, if teams come up with similar impact statements, group those phrases together or mark them with an asterisk. Your task is to summarize in a phrase that reminds everyone of the impact and the underlying story. So for the La Marzocco examples, we might have written down:

• Building the community. (Andrija's coffee shop inspiring new businesses.)

- People feeling more valued and fulfilled in life. (Elisabeth and the coffee farm.)

- People seeing possibility where before they did not. (Emilio becoming head roaster.)

After every team has had the chance to share, bring together all the output you have gathered during the session. That includes the one flip-chart page containing all the verbs/action phrases generated from conversation 2 and the two flip-chart pages with impact statements generated from conversation 3. Position those flip charts at the front of the room so all can see them. You now have everything you need for what comes next: drafting the Why Statement.

Draft a Why Statement

(🕐 35–40 MINUTES)

The next step in the process is for the group to turn the verbs/action phrases and impact statements elicited from the three conversations into a couple of possible versions of a Why Statement. We call these "Candidate Why Statements" because they will later evolve into a single draft statement that the group will carry forward and refine further.

The ability of a group of people to do remarkable things hinges on how well those people can pull together as a team.

_____

How to Write a Why Statement
(⏱ 5 MINUTES)

Of course, the group members can't create a Why Statement if they don't know what one looks like. So your first point of order, as the facilitator, is to show them. Using a flip chart, or a slide, show the group the basic structure of a Why Statement:

TO _____ **SO THAT** _____ .

Explain that although this is not the *only* way to express a WHY, it is the one Simon and the Start With Why team recommend you start with. This is because the blanks capture the two main components of an actionable WHY and the format focuses everyone on what's most important.

Break down the statement into its two main elements. The first element, "To _____," is the contribution the organization or group makes. The second element, "so that _____," is the impact or effect that contribution has on others.

CONTRIBUTION   IMPACT

Many people will immediately recognize the relationship between the output of the three conversations and the anatomy of the Why Statement. But just to be sure you're all on the same page, spell out the relationship for everyone.

Here's what you can tell them: conversation 1 and conversation 2 correspond to the contribution element of the statement; conversation 3 corresponds to the impact element. The words and phrases on the flip charts at the front of the room are the inputs that will fill in the blanks. In this concise Why Statement format, we are describing the world we would like to live in (the impact element) and articulating the action we need to take on Monday morning to bring it to life (the contribution element).

Candidate Why Statement Exercise
(© 25 MINUTES)

Split the group into *two* teams of about the same size. Working independently, each team will write one Candidate Why Statement on a fresh flip-chart page and then present it to the rest of the room. Use the instructions below to give them context before they get started.

First, to write the "contribution" element of the Why Statement each team needs to look at the flip chart in the front of the room that lists all of the verbs and action phrases they came up with earlier. The team members need to decide, together, which verb or action phrase seems to best capture the contribution they make as an organization. This becomes the contribution part of their Candidate Why Statement. It's important for them not to get hung up on the dictionary definition of these verbs and action phrases. It's the *feeling* the words evoke that's important. As they work on this, tell them not to worry about passing over the other themes on the flip chart, some of which they may feel also represent who they are, yet aren't the clear winner. They will come back into play later on when we look at HOWs. For now, each team needs to focus on choosing the verb or action phrase that is first among equals—the one that deeply resonates on a visceral level.

Next, they need to review the impact statements on the other flip charts at the front of the room. From that list they must draw the "impact" part of their Candidate Why Statement.

The goal for each group is to write a Candidate Why Statement that is so inspiring that the other team will say, "Let's go with yours!"

Give the teams twenty-five minutes to write *one* Candidate Why Statement each, reminding them again that they must draw on the words and phrases displayed on the flip charts at the front of the room. It is vital that the statements come from this material. Otherwise, people may fall back on general aspirational language or a branding or marketing position.

FACILITATOR TIP

As the teams start work on this exercise, they may get into a semantic debate about the meaning of certain words. If that happens, refer them back to the stories behind the words and the underlying *feeling*. It is not so much the dictionary definition of the words that matters. What's more important is the deeper meaning these words have for the team.

To help the teams stay on target, tell them that they will each be asked to bring their Candidate Why Statement to life by linking it to two stories represented on the flip charts.

Twenty-five minutes is not a long time for this exercise, but it is enough. We keep it short because we want people to go with their gut (a.k.a. their limbic brain) and not overthink it. After all, the goal at this moment is not to get all the way to a final Why Statement, but to take the first step toward it. We also like to create a little time pressure because it tends to lead people to rely on their emotions. Fear of running out of time encourages them to say, "Oh, what the heck," and just go with what feels right.

Reporting Out: Presenting the Candidate Why Statements
(🕐 5-10 MINUTES)

The team presentations should be short—two minutes maximum per team. Each team should cover the two bullet points below and say no more than that:

• State the WHY (with no explanation or detail)

• Link to two of the stories shared earlier in the workshop that best exemplify the WHY being lived. Doing so ensures the WHY is based on who you actually are and demonstrates that communicating your stories is a great way to share the WHY.

FACILITATOR TIP
As each team presents, ask someone from the other team to film them. Nothing fancy required—a phone or tablet camera will serve just fine. Recording the presentations puts the teams a little more on their game; it also preserves a piece of the Why Discovery experience for future reference.

Once the two teams have presented their Candidate Why Statements, the group may overwhelmingly agree that one statement captures the WHY better than the other. This was very much the case with La Marzocco. In the event of consensus around one Candidate, that statement becomes the *Draft* Why Statement that the group will carry forward. Sometimes, the majority will feel that the WHY can be best expressed by combining the two Candidate Why Statements. Work with them to come to an agreement on a single Draft Why Statement. Remember, no one expects this version to be perfect. As we mentioned earlier, the aim of this workshop is to produce a Why Statement that's 75–80 percent done. That's the reason we call it a draft—we want to keep the conversation going beyond the end of the discovery session.

Once you have arrived at the Draft Why Statement, the teams will probably feel that there's more work to be done. If so, ask for volunteers (we'd suggest a maximum of six) who would like to continue working on the statement. These "Why Champions" should come together over the following couple of weeks to try to refine the words of the Why Statement. It may take time to find the words that feel right. That's normal. The most important thing is for the Draft Why Statement to be actionable.

Here are some examples of Why Statements at different levels of development. The first two are in the correct form: simple and clear, actionable and free of WHATs, focused on service to others and written in affirmative language that resonates with the group:

- To believe in people so that they can, in turn, believe in themselves.

- To provoke people to think differently so that they can be awakened to new possibilities.

Next, here are a couple that are almost there:

- To constantly improve ourselves so that we may be well equipped to overcome the challenges we face.

- To do good in the world, to help people build skills and to learn constantly and have a clear sense of direction/vision, so that they can accomplish much for themselves, their family and their community, effectively and successfully.

Do you see how those two can be improved? The first is about "ourselves" and not about others. The second is about others, but it's way too complex to be remembered, let alone acted upon.

And finally, two more that need quite a bit of work:

- To support our dealers so that they can have sustainable businesses and realize higher profits.

- To help clients manage every aspect of their wealth so that they can rest assured that no stone is unturned in their wealth management.

These statements are both very firmly focused on WHATs rather than WHYs.

Discovering a WHY is as much about the journey as it is about the destination. The process allows us to build the kind of emotional connections to the WHY that will make it genuine, true and long-lasting. Over the months and years that follow your discovery session, it is possible that the words of the organization's Why Statement will change slightly. What should not change is the feeling *behind* the words.

* * *

Wrapping Up the Session
(🕐 10–15 MINUTES)

The Why Discovery process generates a lot of energy. By the end of a session, many people are fired up and motivated to carry the WHY forward. Help them use that momentum. Even if a "final" Draft Why Statement has not yet been agreed upon, dedicate the end of the Why Discovery session to discussing ways participants can put their WHY into practice. Here are some ideas for how to bring the WHY to life in day-to-day business:

- Reward the behavior you want to see. When you see people acting in ways that align with the WHY, acknowledge it and praise them.

- When you make decisions, run your thoughts through a simple filter. Ask, "Does this choice help us move closer to living in alignment to our WHY or not?" Act accordingly.

- Reframe HOWs and WHATs in the context of the WHY. When assigning new tasks or implementing new strategies, make sure people can see *how* those things are expressions of the WHY.

- Be conscious of your leadership. Make it a habit to ask yourself, "What did I do as a leader today that was a tangible manifestation of our WHY?"

- Provide an opportunity for everyone in the organization to discover their own WHY and to learn how it fits within the organization's WHY.

We've shared all the steps we use for conducting a Tribe Why Discovery. As you well know, facilitating is much more than just following steps. It's as much an art as a science. Only through experience will you find the balance that makes this process uniquely yours. Helping tribes find their WHY is one of our favorite things to do. It brings us a great deal of fulfillment. Although we've both done many Why Discoveries, we still get butterflies in our stomachs when we step in front of a room full of people who are eager to find the WHY of their tribe. In these situations, we take a deep breath and source ourselves from a place of being in service to those in the room. Part of being a master facilitator is knowing when to follow the steps and when to trust your intuition. The artful balance is allowing each tribe to find their own path to discovering their WHY.

In Appendix 3 at the end of this book, we've outlined some of the key points for facilitating this session. You might like to refer to it and add your own notes as you prepare to run your first Why Discovery workshop.

Good luck and inspire on!

CHAPTER 6

State Your HOWs

Up to this point we've focused on articulating your Why Statement either as an individual or a tribe. The goal of this chapter is to help you complete your Golden Circle. As a reminder, the Golden Circle consists of three parts: WHY, HOW and WHAT. All three parts are equally important. When those three things are in balance we are at our natural best. We are truly living our WHY. Our WHY is our purpose, cause or belief—the driving force behind everything we do. Our HOWs are the actions we take when we are at our natural best to bring our WHY to life. Our WHATs are the tangible manifestation of our WHY, the actual work we do every day. While other individuals or organizations may express their WHY in a way that is similar to yours, it's HOW you bring your WHY to life that makes you unique. As a result, the combination of your WHY and HOWs is as exclusively yours as your fingerprint.

Like the Why Statement, HOWs are not aspirational. They do not express who we *want* to be. They express the manner in which we actually behave—the things we actually do—when we are at our best. They are the actions we can choose to take on a daily basis to help ensure that we're creating the type of environment in which we thrive.

You've already laid the groundwork for articulating your HOWs, because they are derived from the themes you listed during the Why Discovery process. The themes that didn't end up in your Why Statement will serve as the foundation for your HOWs, which take us from theory to practice.

Your HOWs Are Your Strengths

During either the individual or the tribe Why Discovery process, you identified several themes. These themes are your strengths. It's likely your partner or facilitator helped you uncover themes that you didn't even realize were such a big part of who you are or who your tribe is when at its best. These behaviors were so natural to you that you may have been thinking, "What's the big deal? Isn't that what anyone else would have done in that situation?" The reality is what we hold dear and the way in which we behave in the name of those values can differ wildly from person to person or tribe to tribe. As the partner or facilitator, one of our favorite things is helping people see how unique and world class they truly are—that moment when someone is able to step back, look at the patterns and recognize how spectacularly awesome they are. Your HOWs are the ingredients you need to be at your best. Together, they are your recipe for success—your strengths. And this is true for both an individual and a tribe.

To understand this better, let's look at HOWs from the individual perspective. As social animals, we do not always operate entirely on our own; we need others to survive and thrive. Knowing the WHY and HOWs of those closest to us can be a huge advantage. At Start With Why, we have a culture that focuses on helping people play to their strengths. This doesn't mean that we don't all work hard to raise awareness to our weaknesses, but instead of trying to master something that doesn't come to us naturally, we focus on teaming up in ways that allow us to lean in to the strengths of another.

For example, David's WHY is *to propel people forward so that they can make their mark on the world*. His HOWs are:

- See the big picture
- Take responsibility
- Explore alternative perspectives
- Tie a bow on it (i.e., if you start something, finish it)
- Learn from every experience

Peter's WHY is *to enable people to be extraordinary so that they can do extraordinary things*. His HOWs are:

- Make it simple
- Get up on the balcony (i.e., see the wider context)
- Embrace new ideas
- Build relationships
- Push the boundaries

Our Why Statements are aligned. While the two of us use different words to express our purpose, cause or belief, we both strive to help others to be the best versions of themselves. This alignment makes working together very rewarding for us. However, it's our different strengths, our complimentary HOWs, that allow us to have a far greater impact together than either of us could have alone.

A client once requested we take a hundred and fifty people through a workshop that we generally do with forty. We thought we could do it, but for best results, we felt we needed a full day. This client only had a four-hour window. Our initial reaction was: Impossible! While others may have thrown in the towel right then and there, *we* couldn't help but see this as an opportunity to help one hundred and fifty people become their best selves. (Refer to our Why Statements above!)

To figure out the best way to leverage this opportunity so as to engage and inspire the workshop participants in the allotted time, we put our heads together—or, rather, our HOWs together.

Both of us instinctively wanted to get clear on the situation at hand. David's "see the big picture" and Peter's "get up on the balcony" are similar in nature. We both value strategy before action. It was good we were both strong here because it took both of us to crack the code.

In order to pull this off, we were both going to have to get way out of our comfort zone. We would need to do something we were very familiar with in a very different way.

Though Peter is very good at and open to "embracing new ideas," it was David's ability to "explore alternative perspectives" that saved the day. David is world class at figuring out how to adapt content in completely unconventional ways to ensure that people have a powerful and transformative experience.

Once we had our recipe for success, we had a major challenge. Our recipe was quite complex. The number of moving parts required to deliver this workshop successfully were overwhelming and the details to execute were intricate. How would we convey this to the client? Simple, we'll simplify it. This is where Peter took the lead to "make it simple," ensuring everyone could clearly understand and support the plan. In the end, we were able to deliver our workshop to a much larger audience than usual, which brought us a great deal of fulfillment because we were able to bring our WHYs of propelling people forward and enabling them to be extraordinary to life.

You might be thinking that this sounds a little oversimplified! The truth is, this teaming thing is pretty complex. It's messy, it's unscripted, it's human. That said, our HOWs give us a shared language to see one another's strengths, making it easier to collaborate and lean in to our teammates to get things done. Bottom line is when we focus on our strengths and lean in to the strengths of others, we can make the impossible possible.

**The greatest contribution
of a leader is to
make other leaders.**

——————

HOWs as Filters

When our HOWs are clearly stated, we have a recipe to put ourselves into and create environments where we can be at our natural best. We don't live in a perfect world. While it's not possible to do this in every situation, the name of the game is to seek out and seize the opportunities in which we can each make the greatest possible impact for others and, in turn, feel more fulfilled.

To help ensure that the people we partner with, the projects we take on and the organizations we choose to work in are aligned with our personal values, we can use our HOWs as a filter. Once you've stated your HOWs in a simple, actionable way, it's helpful to add a few bullets to clarify what they mean in practice. This additional detail is useful for you and those with whom you collaborate. Picking back up on the example of an individual, see how Simon does this below.

Simon's HOWs are:

1. Take the unconventional perspective

- See something from a different angle. Open up to doing things a different way.
- Ask, "Is there another, possibly better, way of doing this?"

- Try something. If it doesn't work, try something else.

2. Keep it simple

- When things are simple, everyone can understand. If a ten-year-old can understand what you're saying, you're good to go.
- Simple language and simple ideas are easily understood and easier to execute.

3. Silver line it

- Find something positive in every situation and in every person.

4. Share everything

- Share ideas and feelings. Invite and teach others to share too.
- Share your idea, especially if it's not perfect. Even the "worst" ideas can be built upon.
- Others won't know how you feel or what you want until you share it.

5. Focus on the long term

- Build something that will outlast every one of us.
- Focus on momentum and trending more than hitting arbitrary numbers and dates.

Simon puts his HOWs into daily practice. He uses them to determine whether a new project or opportunity will allow him to live his WHY as fully as possible. Years ago a leader asked Simon if he could help them create an organization that put people first. Right off the bat, Simon liked this leader and the initial proposal piqued his interest. Remember, Simon's WHY is to inspire people to do the things that inspire them so that, together, we can change our world. Simon knows that people-first cultures are more inspiring for employees and customers alike. He also knows that helping an organization change not only their mindset but also their systems and processes to create a people-first organization isn't easy. This collaboration would need to be long term if it were to be successful, so Simon knew he needed to ensure they would be a good fit. Though Simon and this leader were aligned at the WHY level, this is only the first filter.

Simon had a good feeling about this but took the time to ask some questions about how this leader saw this partnership working. Excitedly, the executive presented him with a complex diagram detailing how the initiative would unfold. He explained to Simon that if his board were to invest in this, they'd be looking for quick results.

Immediately red flags popped up. That complex diagram, coupled with a desire for "quick results" would likely not equal long-term progress (see HOW: Focus on the long term). Simon expressed his concern and asked the leader what he meant when he said "quick results." If the board wanted to see things trending in the right direction in the first few months, Simon felt they might be able to find some leading metrics. Simon explained that if he was to collaborate with this leader, that he and his board would need to be open to some wildly new perspectives (see HOW: Take the unconventional perspective). They would need to be open to taking a different approach to effect the desired change than they'd taken before. In the end, it became clear that the complexity (see HOW: Keep it simple), timeline and leadership's mindset were not going to make this a good fit for either party.

This was a big organization, and it was a great opportunity to touch the lives of many people. It was early in Simon's career, and this organization would have looked great on his list of clients. Yet, it just didn't feel right. Simon knew from experience that it was better to sit on the sidelines and cheer on this organization rather than to actively engage in a relationship that was sure to be hard for both of them because he would not be in an environment where he could be at his natural best. Since Simon believed this leader did truly want to make a change in his organization, he introduced him to a few of his contacts whom he thought might be better fits.

Start using your HOWs as filters for making important decisions. Though not every relationship, project or partnership will be in perfect alignment with all your HOWs, you'll have a good idea where challenges or tensions might arise. Knowing these can give you an opportunity to talk about potential issues in advance, giving you and whomever you collaborate with the best possible setup for the partnership to thrive.

It works in reverse too. When you find yourself in a situation where you're frustrated—it "just doesn't feel right" yet you "can't put your finger on it"—use your HOWs to see if you can find out what's out of alignment. Sometimes by simply running down the list of HOWs, you'll immediately be able to put into words what isn't working for you. Once you can put your frustration into words, it makes it easier to ask for what you need to get things back on track.

At Start With Why, we encourage team members experiencing tension to look not only at their Golden Circle but also at the Golden Circle of the colleague they are frustrated with. We have each team member's Golden Circle available for any teammate to look up the WHY and HOWs of any colleague at any time. It's sometimes the case that what is bothering us the most about another is something that is their strength! Seeing this can give us empathy and help us appreciate the gifts of our teammates. It allows us to talk about tension in a common language, which allows us to move through tensions quickly. Like most tools, the more you practice talking about your HOWs and using them as tools, the more adept you become with them.

Corporate Values Versus HOWs

The underlying process for expressing an organization's HOWs is very similar to the individual approach. A tribe's HOWs are its guiding principles, derived from the themes that emerged during the Why Discovery process. And yet, very often when we are brought in to do a Tribe Why Discovery, the organization already has a socialized set of values. In many cases, even though the values may be written in big letters on the wall, we are able to quickly assess that few people actually know what they mean. If you ask a handful of people at different levels of the organization what their core value "integrity" means and you hear a handful of different answers, that is your sign.

Many of us have worked for a company that listed its core values on every conference room wall. Included were such garden-variety buzzwords as "honesty," "hard work," "diversity" and, yes, "integrity." These values are all fine and good. But they are not HOWs.

Most companies don't ground their core values in an understanding of how the organization performs when at its best. Core values are generally aspirational. They express the qualities the company would *like* its employees to embody rather than those it actually displays. Remember, HOWs are not aspirational. They do not express who we *want* to be. They express the ways we actually behave—the things we actually do—when we are at our best.

The other difference between HOWs and core values is that values are not, in and of themselves, actions. "Courtesy" is a value. "Treat people with kindness and respect" is a HOW. The distinction is even more important when the applications of a core value are not immediately apparent. Imagine someone coming to work on their first day of a new job and seeing a poster of the company's core values in the cafeteria. Seeing the word "integrity," they might think, "Okay, sure. But what do you want me to do?" Now imagine that same employee is given a copy of the company's Why Statement and sees the HOW "Always tell the truth." Then later that day at the training they hear their supervisor say, "We do not misrepresent the effectiveness of our product even to make a sale." In this case they'd probably say, "Got it! I can do that." If we expect people to live the core values of an organization, we have to be able to tell them what those values look like in action. In other words, the HOWs must be simple and actionable.

Sometimes we meet with the leadership of the organization and for various reasons they are attached to their current list of values. It could be that it's been socialized for so long they think it would be inauthentic to just change them out of the blue. It could be that they just spent millions of dollars to have a big firm help them come up with and roll out their values and changing them would feel wishy washy. Whatever the reason, if you find yourself in that situation, we suggest going through the Tribe Approach process exactly as advised in chapters 4 and 5, then use the themes discovered to add some color to the corporate values they already have. You likely will find a few clear intersections of what they already have and the themes you found. Help them make a deeper and more meaningful connection where things naturally come together.

Your HOWs Bring Your WHY to Life

In the late 1950s, Enrique Uribe, who lived in Costa Rica, decided to import an idea that had revolutionized grocery shopping in the United States. In Costa Rica, people were accustomed to going into a store and asking the person behind the counter for what they needed—a kilo of flour, a liter of cooking oil, a loaf of bread. The assistant would measure out the flour from a large sack and the oil from a drum and bring them to the customer. That had long been the system in the United States as well, but now it was different. Self-service markets, which had become the norm in the States, set the entire range of products on display and left it up to customers to collect what they wanted and bring the items to the counter. This new way of shopping meant that more choices could be offered and more customers could be served. Enrique wanted this to be the future of shopping in Costa Rica as well, but, like anyone with a new idea that bucks tradition, he encountered resistance.

People had various reasons for ridiculing Enrique's vision. Some predicted an increase in shoplifting. Others simply preferred the personal service of having a clerk do the work of rounding up all the items. Others pointed out that the entire supply chain would have to be reinvented. Products could no longer arrive in vats and sacks; they would have to be individually packaged. And stores would have to maintain greater inventory.

In 1960, Enrique, together with his siblings Marta, Flory and Luis, opened Mas x Menos, a supermarket that brought to life his vision of a new way of shopping. And people liked it. As Mas x Menos grew to become the largest retail chain in the country, with over five hundred stores, it completely reshaped the market. (Pun intended.)

Enrique's sons, Rodrigo and Carlos, carried forward their father's passion for innovation. Though they eventually sold the family supermarket chain, the brothers went on to found Cuestamoras, a parent company to more than a dozen businesses reaching into health, hospitality, urban development and energy. But as Cuestamoras grew over the years, Rodrigo and Carlos, who serve as the chairman and vice chairman of the board, came to recognize they had a problem.

As a parent to so many businesses in so many different industries, Cuestamoras was in danger of losing touch with what the brothers felt their company stood for—its founding purpose. This is very common among companies that expand beyond their original product or service. They become so focused on *what* they are doing, they lose touch with *why* they started and *how* they should continue. So in 2014, the Uribe brothers set out to properly articulate the company's WHY, to find the golden thread that connects everything it does now to everything that came before. By going through the Individual Why Discovery process, the brothers identified Cuestamoras's overarching purpose: *to innovate relentlessly in order to create opportunities for everyone.*

They also identified and articulated the HOWs they rely on to make decisions and run their businesses:

- Break new ground
- Embrace change
- Learn with a humble mind
- Do what is right
- Work together

Now the company places great value on executing its HOWs with a high degree of *discipline*. While their WHATs are diverse, they approach every new project by following what they call the Cuestamoras System. Step one is to ask, "Will doing this project help us bring our WHY to life?" If the answer is yes, the company then makes sure to stick to its HOWs all along the way as the project develops.

Although the family business has changed and greatly expanded since the 1950s, Enrique's true legacy lives on through his sons, because they have rediscovered his WHY—rooted in that first Mas x Menos store—and reinforced it with the values and behaviors that are aligned with those of the founder. As long as that WHY and those HOWs remain front and center, it doesn't matter how many businesses or industries Rodrigo and Carlos enter into. However greatly they alter their company's WHATs, they will continue to inspire in the long term.

Elephant Trap: Before you identify your own HOWs, a quick caution. The sample HOWs you've read about in this chapter relate to specific people and organizations. Guard against thinking that your HOWs need to be the same or similar. They don't! Your HOWs will come from the stories you or your group shared during the Why Discovery process. That is what makes them authentic and real rather than a catchphrase that was cooked up just to sound good.

* * *

Here is your road map for the process of articulating your HOWs. The template is the same for both individuals and tribes.

NARROW REMAINING THEMES **STATE YOUR HOWs** **PROVIDE CONTEXT**

The HOWs Process

When you went through the process of discovering your WHY, you identified a number of themes in the stories you told. One or two of these themes—the ones that resonated most—were incorporated in your Why Statement. The rest of the themes have been sitting there waiting for you to do something with them. Now is that time. The remainder of this chapter is dedicated to showing you how to turn those remaining themes into HOWs by following the three steps, outlined below.

Narrow Remaining Themes

Take your list of themes and cross out the ones you channeled into your Why Statement. Then narrow the remaining list of themes until you have no more than five. Why five rather than six? There's no science behind this. It's just that in the thousands of times we've done this process, we have consistently found that the themes can be successfully boiled down to a maximum of five separate and distinct ideas. Sometimes there are only four, but never more than five. We'll show you how to focus your themes below. Since the Tribe Approach leaves you with a list of active verbs (e.g., to embrace the unknown, to protect, to connect), we will use an example of how an individual would work through the process because their themes may still need some additional work. A tribe follows the same process.

After drafting a Why Statement, this person had eight more themes on their list:

- Joy
- Optimistic
- Connection
- Feeling of safety
- Always learned from others
- There's always a solution
- Protected loved ones
- Problem solving

First, look for themes that express similar ideas. Once you identify these overlaps or redundancies, you have two options—keep one and cross out the other *or* combine them to create a new theme. In the example above, "Protected loved ones" and "Feeling of safety" are very close in essence. If one *felt* more right that the other, that's the one we'd keep. In this case, we come up with a phrase that draws on both: "Making others feel safe."

Another overlap was "There's always a solution" and "Problem solving." Again, we would keep one or combine them. Here, it felt right to keep "There's always a solution."

Similarly, another pair was "Joy" and "Optimistic." A dictionary would define these words differently, but remember, for the purposes of the discovery exercise, we are guided not by the dictionary but by *referring back to the stories that inspired these themes in the first place.* In this case, they chose to hold on to "Optimistic."

We now have a final list of five:

- Optimistic
- Connection
- Making others feel safe
- Always learned from others
- There's always a solution

Narrow remaining themes

1. _____

2. _____

3. _____

4. _____

5. _____

State Your HOWs

As we explained earlier, HOWs must be actions because they are the things you *do* to bring your WHY to life. Traits and attributes, such as "honesty," or adjectives, such as "determined," are not actions. We turn themes into HOWs by making them actionable. It's possible that some of your themes will already be in the form of a verb or action, which is great. For those that are traits or adjectives, here's how to proceed.

Consider one of the themes from our example list above:

• Optimistic

There are various ways to transform the adjective "optimistic" into a HOW. Here are just a few possibilities:

• Find the positive in everything
• See the glass as half full
• Look forward, not backward
• Find the silver lining in every cloud

After digging into the stories, we agreed that "Find the positive in everything" really embodied what they meant when we wrote down the theme "Optimistic."

The other themes in the list are pretty close and just need a tweak in order to become actions:

- Connection ➔ Connect with people in meaningful ways
- Making others feel safe ➔ Make others feel safe
- Always learned from others ➔ Learn something from everyone
- There's always a solution ➔ Look for creative solutions

Notice how the simple shift in language turns these passive words or phrases into actions we can actually perform on a daily basis.

Here's the final list of HOWs from our example:

- Find the positive in everything
- Connect with people in meaningful ways
- Make others feel safe
- Learn something from everyone
- Look for creative solutions

We have a few personal preferences we'll share with you. We don't like to use "Be" verbs, because they don't feel active to us. We can feel the difference between "Be connected" and "Connect with people in meaningful ways" or "Be positive" and "Find the positive in everything." We also advise you to drop the gerund. Take the "ing" off of your verbs. It's more inclusive and a clearer instruction. "Making others feel safe" versus "Make others feel safe."

There are exceptions to every rule and the most important thing to remember is that if it feels right, it is right.

Make sure the words you use resonate with you and remind you of the stories behind them. It's this emotional connection that will inspire you to put these HOWs into action.

State Your HOWs

1. _____

2. _____

3. _____

4. _____

5. _____

Provide Context

Once you've articulated your HOWs, you can strengthen your relationship to them by writing a short description that gives each one some context and suggests what it might look like in practice. The descriptions don't have to be complicated. In fact, keep them as simple as you can. That makes them easier to put into action.

Here are what descriptions to the HOWs looked like for this individual:

- Find the positive in everything—When things look like they're going wrong, look for what's going right.
- Connect with people in meaningful ways—Make relationships personal and let people know you care about them.
- Make others feel safe—Extend trust to others and let people know you have their back.
- Learn something from everyone—Be open to the ideas and points of view of others; they all have something to teach us.
- Look for creative solutions—Assume there is always a solution and don't give up until you find it.

We've included some examples of Tribe Why Discoveries we've facilitated at the end of this chapter. We've shared the step-by-step process by which they turned their themes into HOWs.

Provide context to your HOWs by adding short descriptions to each:

1. _____

2. _____

3. _____

4. _____

5. _____

And finally, make a note of your WHATs:

1. _____

2. _____

3. _____

* * *

Congratulations. By figuring out the WHY and HOWs behind your WHATs, you have completed your individual or tribe Golden Circle. As you begin to start with WHY and share your vision and values with others, use the stories from the Why Discovery process—the energy and emotions evoked by those stories is the key to being able to authentically communicate what you stand for.

More Tribe Examples

Here's an actual example of a Golden Circle from a Tribe Why Discovery for a small team:

Original list of action phrases:

- To educate
- To enable
- To direct
- To mentor
- To inspire
- To collaborate

These words and action phrases were expressed as these themes:

To connect, to educate, to support, to collaborate, to instill confidence, to inspire possibility.

From these themes came the team's WHY:

"To connect and engage so that people feel empowered in their lives."

And then their HOWs:

- We educate and enlighten
- We support and direct
- We enhance collaboration
- We instill confidence
- We inspire possibility

And, to complete the picture, here are their WHATs:

- We build people's relationship to information to enable them to make better decisions.
- We give confidence to engage in IT issues and make IT choices.
- We take the lead on investment decisions that affect the company's ability to deliver.
- We develop apps that include the wider community that would otherwise be excluded.
- We design and implement systems to enable people to communicate effectively, avoiding disruption.
- We bring together strategy and IT planning to ensure the future of our business makes sense.
- We support the communications infrastructure that supports us.
- We bring communities together, inside and outside of the company.
- We inform and inspire people through the possibilities of IT.

Here's another Golden Circle example, this one created by a team consisting of fewer than ten people:

Original list of verbs and action phrases:

- To motivate
- To reassure
- To support
- To create
- To innovate
- To inspire

These were translated into these themes:

To feel safe, to support, to celebrate differences, to listen and recognize, to be open, to collaborate.

From these themes came their WHY:

"To hold the space so that together we can find the courage to challenge our boundaries."

And their HOWs:

- We support one another
- We celebrate differences
- We recognize small things
- We foster openness
- We bring together talent

Interestingly, after the members of this group discovered their WHY and HOWs, they didn't feel the need to write much about their WHATs:

- Design
- Branding
- Software engineering
- Astronomy

CHAPTER 7

Take a Stand

Do the Things You Say You Believe

Taking the time to discover our WHY and articulate our HOWs is simply how we begin the journey. Next comes the hard part. We have to act on them. We have to bring them to life. We have to share them.

Share Your WHY

Just knowing our WHY doesn't mean we instantly feel comfortable sharing it. In fact, most of us have been communicating with our WHATs—as we've been shown to do—for our whole lives. It's what we've been taught. It's what has been modeled to us. You may find it a serious challenge to communicate your purpose, cause or belief to others. If so, you're not alone!

Remember learning to ride a bike? You felt awkward at first. Each time you got back on, you focused on a different tactic all the while trying to stay balanced. You were lifting your feet at different times, trying the brakes at various pressures and struggling to look where you wanted to go, all the while preoccupied by what your limbs should be doing. It's likely you fell off a few times, but you got back on the bike and tried again . . . and again . . . and again. And soon you were flying down the road without even thinking about it. Starting with WHY is no different. Once you get the hang of it, it's as natural as riding a bike.

We find that the best place to practice is among strangers. When meeting someone for the first time, they almost always ask, "What do you do?" This is your opportunity to start with WHY. From this point forward, strangers on planes, chitchatters at cocktail parties and everyone in between represent your metaphorical bicycle.

While you can recite your Why Statement word for word, you can also try variations of your statement and stories to help it give meaning to others. Simon, for example, might say, "I inspire people to do things that inspire them, so that, together, we can change our world." This is his Why Statement word for word. He sometimes says, "I work with leaders to build inspiring organizations that put people first. I believe that if enough organizations do this, we will change our world." He often uses our vision statement to begin a conversation. If he's talking about Start With Why, our organization, he'll say, "We imagine a world where the vast majority of people wake up inspired to go to work, feel safe when they are there and return home at the end of the day fulfilled by the work they do. Every product we make, every partnership we have and everything we do is to bring this vision to life." You get the idea. It's not about using the exact words of your Why Statement, though that's a good place to start. It's about finding ways to share who you are and what you stand for.

If the first couple of times you try this and you don't get the reaction you were hoping for, don't let that discourage

DANGER! DANGER!: Once you know your WHY, you have a choice to live it every day. Living it means consistently taking actions that are in alignment with the things you say. If you say one thing and do another too frequently, you will lose the trust of others. Our actions either add to or take away from the trust and loyalty others feel toward us. When the things we say and the things we do are aligned with what we believe, we are fully living our WHY. Will you choose to take a stand?

you. We both shared some embarrassing tales of our first attempts of starting with WHY while writing this chapter. It's always easier to look back and laugh after you've mastered a skill. We don't know anyone who has escaped the early days of getting up the courage to share their WHY only to have the person they're talking to look at them like they have three heads. That's falling off the bike! It's going to happen. If that's the reaction you get, it means one of two things.

It could mean that you weren't very clear. What you meant to say and what actually came out of your mouth were not aligned. Like riding a bike, where you wanted to go and where you ended up weren't always the same place. It could also be the case that everything came out perfectly but didn't resonate with the person you were talking to. Remember, the WHY is a filter. When you start with WHY, it attracts people who believe what you believe and repels people who don't. The person who politely ends the conversation or switches topics is probably someone with whom your WHY does not resonate. That's perfectly fine. You don't want to spend a bunch of time small talking with someone who doesn't believe what you believe. It's just a sign that there is someone else with whom you could be having a deep and meaningful conversation. Go find them!

Share the Tribe's WHY

(⏱ 3-4 HOURS)

One of the most effective ways to share within an organization is to create an opportunity for others to hear about and feel inspired by the WHY. Then they can take ownership of it and put it into practice. If your tribe is large enough that not everyone could be included in the Why Discovery process, what is the best way to share it with everyone else? If you are the founder of the organization and have discovered your WHY and now want to share it with your tribe, how can you get started?

Below is an approach we have used to help people share the WHY with fellow tribe members who were not part of the discovery process. You can also use this approach to onboard new employees or partners, ensuring that the tribe's WHY stays alive as the organization grows. It's a

SHARE THE EXPERIENCE   **HELP OTHERS OWN THE WHY**   **EXPLORE NEW OPPORTUNITIES**

simple three-step process, conducted with fifty people at a time in a workshop lasting three to four hours. The facilitator of your Tribe Why Discovery process could be a good candidate to run this workshop too. Here's the road map: Each step is a facilitated conversation held in a setting similar to the one recommended for the Tribe Why Discovery in chapter 4.

Facilitator Section

Who Should Attend?

We recommend that participants in this workshop volunteer to attend. In the early stages of the Why Discovery rollout, you want the early adopters, the people who are interested and excited about participating. Remember the Law of Diffusion of Innovation that Simon talks about in *Start with Why*, which says that early adopters of innovations will then enthusiastically spread them to others? If it's possible, start with those people who are most enthusiastic about the Why Discovery work. Early adopters will help you socialize the idea throughout the organization. It will be faster and cheaper to use this approach versus a formal corporate top-down rollout. In the end, it may be formally rolled out even though it's not the ideal first step in socializing the idea.

See chapter 7 in *Start with Why* for more on this topic.

If you find yourself in a situation where you need to have a few people in the room who don't check the early adoptors box, but who do need to "get on board" or "buy in" in order for things to move forward, that's okay. Do your best to ensure the majority of participants are eager to be a part of this new and exciting milestone of the organization.

Step 1: Share the Experience
(⏱ 60–75 MINUTES)

Begin the workshop by reviewing the Golden Circle and the concept of WHY. Some participants may have already heard something about these ideas; others will be starting from zero. Everyone in the room needs to develop a foundational understanding of what it means to start with WHY. An easy way to begin is to show them Simon's TED talk video (http://bit.ly/GoldenCircleTalk). Alternatively, you can review the concept with them yourself—free slides and notes are available at http://bit.ly/FYWresources.

After you review the Golden Circle, invite one or two team members who participated in the Why Discovery process to talk about it. Explain to them in advance that they should not start by revealing the Why Statement straight off. Instead, they should convey to their colleagues how the discovery experience *felt*. Let these team members do the majority of the talking. But in case you need to help them get rolling (or keep rolling), here are some questions to tuck in your back pocket. Pick and choose the ones you like and feel free to add your own.

- Tell us what happened during the Why Discovery session.

- What were some of the stories colleagues shared that particularly resonated with you?

- What were some of the high points of the session?

- How did the group respond?

- What did you learn about your organization or coworkers that you didn't know before?

- How does what you heard during the session make you feel about working here?

- What inspired you most about the Why Discovery process?

As your speakers get going, the other members of the group will probably want to ask them questions as well. Encourage everyone to do so, and let the conversation flow. The more the group engages in the discussion, the more they will understand the value of the WHY and the more they will contribute to the workshop.

There's no time limit to this part of the exercise. So don't rush it. Read the energy in the room. When the interaction reaches a natural stopping point—which could be fifteen minutes after you start, or thirty minutes, or more—you can move on to step 2.

Step 2: Help Others Own the WHY
(⏱ 45–60 MINUTES)

Now for the big reveal: you'll soon be sharing the Why Statement drafted at the discovery session. The best way to begin is by introducing the composition of the statement:

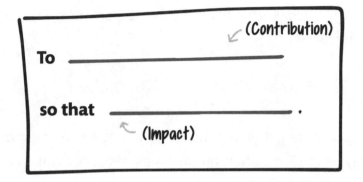

Explain that the Why Statement the tribe members will soon see was discovered (not created) via the themes that emerged from the stories their colleagues shared. Show the flip chart from the Why Discovery where the Candidate words and phrases were recorded. Talk about the process by which you helped whittle these down to a single Why Statement. Retell participants' specific stories whenever that seems helpful. These stories will help bring the WHY to life. If you still have the flip-chart pages from the Why Discovery process or even pictures of them, now would be a great time to share them. Seeing those marked up pages with words crossed out and themes circled can help everyone who wasn't there get an idea of how it all came together.

If every member of a team doesn't grow together they will grow apart.

────────

When you finally arrive at the flip-chart page that reveals the Why Statement, read it out loud and then give the group a chance to take it in.

This moment is where things can get a little tricky. People can get hung up on the words rather than the meaning and feeling behind the words. We recommend taking a few moments here to let everyone know that the words aren't perfect. This is just the first iteration or an early iteration of the Why Statement. Let them know that sometimes the words used in a Why Statement may change a little over time, although the feeling behind the WHY does not. Encourage them to withhold their critiques of the specific language, for now, and to focus instead on what the WHY might look like in action. See if you can get everyone to agree that they have a shared sense—a feeling—for the WHY, even if its articulation is not, in their minds, 100 percent perfect. This will help you avoid semantic quicksand and keep the momentum going.

We have experienced situations when the WHY simply didn't resonate with one or two people in the room. Some of the common reasons for this are that:

- In the past, the organization hasn't always lived its WHY.

- The WHY doesn't align with what the organization and/or the team members have agreed on as their current strategy.

- Sometimes team members feel it's right but don't believe all employees will get behind the WHY, so they feel the need to change it.

- Occasionally, a team member who doesn't resonate with the WHY isn't a great fit for the company.

- If the majority of the room isn't on board with the Why Statement, there is a good chance it needs more refining.

If everyone is not in consensus about the WHY, that's okay. Your goal is not to convince everyone to buy in, but to provide an environment in which they have the opportunity to be inspired by it. Remember, the whole idea behind articulating the WHY is so that we can work together to make positive change in the world.

Now that everyone has a good understanding of the WHY and its underlying themes and stories, they are ready to be split into groups to carry on the conversation. Ideally, each group will include three to eight people. The groups should be small enough that an effective exchange of ideas can happen. Each group needs to report back to the room at the end of this section, so make sure you don't have too many groups.

One way to encourage ownership of the WHY is to have each group share personal experiences that support it. Here are some prompts to get them started:

- Tell a specific story about the reason you *love* working in this organization. Share a story of when you felt proud to be a part of *this* tribe.

- What about the story you just shared validates our WHY?

- Who in our organization best embodies our WHY?

Give each group its own flip chart and have the participants write down their answers to each of these questions as a list of short sentences or phrases, with an emphasis on *stories*. Just as in the Why Discovery session, the stories that carry the most meaning will be the ones that are the most *specific* and *human*.

Allow at least twenty to thirty minutes for this exercise. More often than not, you'll need to bring the segment to a close due to lack of time, not due to a lack of conversation among the participants. After you call a halt, have each group report on their discussion to the rest of the team. That should take about five to seven minutes per group.

When people get passionate about how their personal experiences line up with the WHY, it means they are starting to take ownership of it, which reinforces their connection to the work and to each other. Channel the energy generated by this exercise into the final piece of the workshop.

Step 3: Explore New Opportunities
(🕐 45 MINUTES)

Our WHY comes from our past, but its value and promise lie in the future. An inspiring, clearly articulated WHY acts as a springboard for new and different ways an organization can move forward. Using our tribe's WHY to take us into the future is the focus of the final part of this workshop. We call this a "Conversation of Possibility."

This is the time for participants to throw out ideas about how the organization, guided by its WHY, can advance in new or different ways. This is more than your average brainstorming session. You know that kind of brainstorming session we're talking about, where we begin thinking big until one of us starts anticipating obstacles and challenges, and within three minutes most of us are convinced the new big idea is impossible. "Resource constraints" is one popular bogeyman; you can no doubt think of others. Sadly, when we do this we stall our ideas before they even get started and prevent ourselves from taking action. We limit our progress to small steps, when we could be taking giant leaps. A Conversation of Possibility keeps us away from that excessively safe path. It gives us permission to change our thinking and an opportunity to get out of our own way.

Divide participants into the same groups as before. Explain that in a Conversation of Possibility, resource constraints do not apply. Encourage participants to share any and all ideas—after all, you never know where they will lead. We've seen people bring up an idea they themselves advertised in advance as stupid and then watch as the group transformed it into something everyone was eager to implement. The bigger the ideas the better. Nothing is off the table. Nothing is impossible. Nothing is "stupid." At the same time, make sure everyone understands that a Conversation of Possibility is just that— a conversation. If you surface an idea and it's well received, that does *not* imply that you are now committed to taking it forward. If people fear that offering a suggestion will stick them with making it a reality, they may keep their most ambitious ideas to themselves. It's important to state that a Conversation of Possibility is full of possibility yet requires no commitment.

There are just two rules for this exercise:

- Every idea must align with the WHY.

- Group members can add new ideas or build on someone else's. They cannot say, "No way," "That won't work" or "We can't do that"—that's not the conversation we're in.

To get things started, instruct the groups to answer this question:

- Knowing this is our WHY, what could be possible *inside* our organization? (For example, think about what systems and processes might be modified or introduced.)

The idea here is to get the team looking inward. Remember we must practice what we preach. We must be what we say we are. This is the opportunity to ensure the things we say and the things we do inside the organization are a reflection of who we truly are. People on the inside should first live the WHY for each other, after that, they can focus on how the WHY affects those on the outside. Many organizations want to go directly to a client or product focus. Encourage them to stay in an internal conversation first, and assure them we'll get to the WHATs next. The question above can get them started.

After ten minutes or so, throw out a new question:

- Given the WHY of this organization, what other WHATs are possible? (For example, think about what else we could offer by way of products or services, or the way we communicate with the people we serve.)

So often, organizations get comfortable providing their core offerings and don't consider what other products, services or partnerships could help them live their WHY. (If Apple had done that, none of us would have iPhones, iPads or iTunes.) By specifically asking participants to explore new products or services, this question aims to inspire them to realize that a product can be wildly different from their current offering and still be 100 percent compatible with the organization's WHY.

The groups should write their thoughts on their flip charts. After twenty to thirty minutes, ask them to report to the room. As people hear what the other groups have to say, they may be inspired to think of even more possibilities. It's like climbing the staircase of a tall tower—as you take each step, more comes into view.

To complete the Conversation of Possibility, ask if anyone would like to make a commitment to carry forward the work of the WHY. Specifically, you should ask for commitments to:

- Be "Why Champions" who will keep the WHY alive every day by living it and sharing it with others.

- Take any of the possibilities identified by the team and turn them into action.

- If the HOWs haven't been stated as recommended in chapter 6, it would be ideal for volunteers to identify the organization's HOWs by exploring other themes that emerged during the Why Discovery.

The goal is that by the end of this workshop, team members who had no part in the discovery process will be starting to take ownership of the WHY, which releases energy and inspiration. Each participant will have started to bring the WHY alive with stories of their own. The more they talk about it, the more the WHY starts to take hold. This is how to begin to scale the power of WHY.

* * *

Live Your WHY

Communicating our WHY is an essential part of identifying the people in the world who believe what we believe, who will be our trusted friends, loyal clients or customers, dedicated employees and inspired partners in bringing our WHY to life. That's huge. And it's only the beginning.

For an individual, finding their WHY may lead them to realize that there is something else they could be doing or somewhere else they could be doing it that would likely leave them feeling more fulfilled. Finding an organization's WHY can lead to a similar conclusion. Maybe the organization should be offering a different product or service. Maybe it should reconsider its hiring process or its metrics for progress. Perhaps certain employees would do better in different positions or divisions. Or maybe they simply aren't the right fit at all.

After discovering the WHY and articulating the HOWs it's easier to see which team members, strategies, policies, procedures, systems, products and internal and external communications are in or out of alignment with your core beliefs. If the initial list of things you'd like to change is pretty long, that's normal. It doesn't mean that you have to make immediate or drastic changes. Allow your WHY and HOWs to settle a bit before you move forward in a new direction. Build the relationship to them as you consider how they might shape your next steps. If you decide a change feels right based on what you've learned about yourself and your organization, start small and move forward with confidence.

Remember, the times we feel most fulfilled are the times we are living our WHY. It has always been that way; we just couldn't put it into words. Now you can share your WHY and act on it intentionally. When you keep your WHY on a piece of paper in a drawer, you have a piece of paper in a drawer. When you *live* your WHY, you thrive and so do the people around you.

* * *

Keep the WHY Alive

Peter recently flew Southwest Airlines from St. Louis, Missouri, to Columbus, Ohio. The flight was packed, and the overhead bins were full. As the final passengers boarded, they were instructed to leave their carry-on bags in the forward galley for loading into the baggage hold. Peter could see the flight attendant working hard to make sure each bag was properly labeled for transfer.

This is not an unusual scene on domestic flights. It's what happened next that was surprising. As Peter watched, the plane's captain peered around the flight-deck door and caught sight of the flight attendant labeling bags and then carrying them onto the Jetway for loading. Immediately, and without hesitation, the captain climbed out of his seat and started to help. Peter was amazed. There's a pretty sharp line drawn between flight-deck crew and cabin crew on airlines these days, yet here was a senior captain crossing that line to help another member of the Southwest team ensure that the passengers' bags would make it to where they had to go. By his actions, by his tone in speaking to the flight attendant and by the way he handled the bags, this captain demonstrated to everyone watching that he cared. Peter looked up at the airline's crest on the bulkhead, which bears the outline of a heart at its center, and smiled. He had just witnessed their WHY in action.

For more about Southwest, read chapter 5 of *Start with Why*.

Southwest Airlines is a company that builds its business around a belief in caring for its employees, who in turn care for their customers. In *Start with Why*, Simon cited the airline as an example of an organization that thinks, acts and communicates by starting with WHY. As we write this book seven years later, it seems that Southwest's WHY remains alive and kicking.

* * *

For more on the "split," read chapter 12 in *Start with Why*.

To keep the WHY alive over time, we must keep it front and center, communicating it and committing to living it—on purpose, with purpose—every day. Otherwise, a WHY can fizzle, fade or be forgotten. In an organization, when the WHY goes fuzzy, we call this the "split."

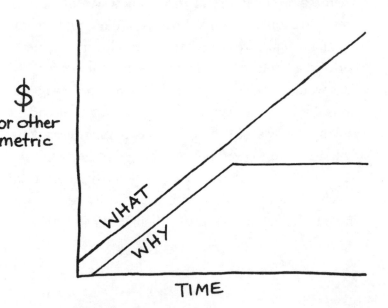

Every organization's development, growth or results can be measured on two axes. The first is time and the second is another metric, usually revenue. When an organization is founded, *what* it does is inextricably linked with *why* it does what it does, even if the company can't express its WHY in words. As the organization grows, its WHAT and WHY grow hand in hand. But as the business scales over time and more and more people are hired, that's when the split becomes a real threat.

In the beginning, when an organization is small, the founder makes the initial hires and directly shares their vision with the team. The entire tribe is often working from the same office; if not, they generally are in daily contact. Employees are inspired by the founder's vision and excited to come to work. They give the organization everything they've got, even if the pay is low and the hours are long. Under these circumstances, the WHY remains alive and well.

As the organization gets bigger, things begin to change. The original founder assigns someone to hire and manage some of the staff. Eventually a management structure is put in place to handle the growth. The person who was hired to hire people now hires someone else to help with this task. After a while, those being hired are further and further removed from the founder and the reason the organization does what it does. The newer hires instinctively start to focus on the more easily measurable WHAT and soon the WHY becomes fuzzy. The point at which this occurs   when the WHY goes fuzzy and the focus shifts to the WHAT—is the split.

Although we may not be able to articulate the change, we can all recognize when our organization experiences the split. Symptoms include increased stress, decreased passion and lower productivity, engagement and innovation. People start saying things like "It used to feel like a family around here. Now it just feels like a job." Whereas people were formerly inspired to stay with the organization, now executives and upper management must actively work to retain them, using tactics such as salary increases, bonuses tied to delivery and share options available only to individuals who'll commit to five more years with the organization. This kind of money-based manipulation can work in the short term but inevitably fails in the long run. Eventually, employee trust and loyalty break down, performance suffers, numbers drop, layoffs begin and the entire culture of the organization begins to erode.

Any organization, even one with a great WHY-based culture, can find itself at the split if it loses focus on the reason it does what it does. Being aware of the problem, however, means that you, as an organization, can guard against it.

Ultimate Software offers a perfect example of how an organization can fend off the split. It is not only experiencing explosive growth, but also has a thriving "people first" culture. The company is a regular in *Fortune*'s 100 Best Companies to Work For list. In 2017, it was number seven on that list and was also voted number two in *People* magazine's Companies That Care list.

In early 2014, they asked us to get involved—not because they were experiencing the split but because they wanted to inoculate themselves against it. They asked us to help them design leadership training that would ensure their leaders had everything they needed so they could always choose to do the right thing.

The leadership team at Ultimate Software knows their WHY: *To provide for people so that they thrive and feel empowered to always do the right thing.* They use that WHY to shape the organization's culture and they envision its future through that lens. Their WHY is not just corporate wallpaper. They live it and breathe it. And they are hypervigilant in protecting it. Ultimate Software prevents the split from happening by consciously, continuously and relentlessly aligning WHAT they do with WHY they do it—and they are succeeding beautifully.

* * *

Whether you are proactively protecting a thriving, long-lived WHY or need to resuscitate a WHY that has been neglected or ignored, one of the most powerful tools at your disposal is also the simplest: storytelling. This is true whether you are an organization or an individual.

Storytelling is the way knowledge and understanding have been passed down for millennia, since long before the invention of written language. Storytelling is part of what it is to be human. And the best stories share our values and beliefs. Those stories are powerful. Those stories inspire. Those stories are both the source of our WHY and the fuel that keeps our WHY alive. That's the reason companies that understand the importance of living their WHY make it easy for their teams to fortify themselves with stories.

Throughout this book, we have talked about the importance of stories for the discovery process. Your WHY comes from your stories—the moments in your life when you felt most fulfilled, the moments when you were your very best self. The more you act intentionally on your WHY, the more of these satisfying stories you will collect. And those stories will deepen your relationship to your WHY and inspire you to keep going. In turn, you'll inspire others.

Inspire On

We mentioned several times that we find facilitating Why Discoveries to be the most fulfilling and inspiring work we do. It's one thing to discover your own WHY, it's another thing to help someone discover theirs. We recommend you do both!

Our team at Start With Why is working hard to build a world where the vast majority of people wake up inspired to go to work, feel safe when they are there and return home at the end of the day fulfilled by the work they do. We are working hard to ensure that every employee has a Golden Circle on their desk and every organization can clearly articulate their higher purpose, cause or belief. This book is just one of the things we are doing to help bring our WHY to life. We know we can't do this alone. Thank you for joining the movement, for helping us share the WHY. Inspire on!

Frequently Asked Questions

We've had the privilege to work with thousands of people in our workshops, and they've asked good questions. It might be fair to assume that, since WHY is our passion, all the answers were on the tips of our tongues. Some were, but some really challenged us, and thinking them through deepened, expanded and clarified our own understanding of WHY. We thought it would add value to this book if we shared the most commonly raised workshop questions, along with our responses. We especially recommend that facilitators read this section, since they may receive similar questions from Tribe Why Discovery participants.

For Individuals

Can my WHY be my family?

Family inspires great love and commitment, and most of us want very much to care for our spouse or partner and our children. But a WHY is who we are *wherever* we are— not just at home, but also at work or out with friends. Though it may seem strange to speak in these terms, family is actually a WHAT. Your WHY will come not from talking about your family, but from talking about the feelings your family evokes in you. During the Why Discovery process, you will inevitably find that the contribution you make to your family members and the impact it has on them are the same contribution you will make and impact you will have on others in any situation that brings out your best self. The bottom line is your family is not your WHY. The reason your best friend loves you is the same reason your significant other loves you, and it's the same reason your best client or colleagues love you too.

Can I have more than one WHY?

Nope. Each of us has one WHY and one WHY only. The WHY is the one common thread that brings out the best in us and makes us feel the most fulfilled. As Simon often says, "If you're different at work than you are at home, in one of those two places you're lying." Who we are at our core does not change depending on where we find ourselves. We either live in alignment with our WHY or we do not. If you feel as if you have one WHY at work and a different one at home (or in some other context), you may be focusing too much on *what* you are doing at each respective place. Instead, think about the common factors at home and at work that leave you feeling inspired and fulfilled. That's where you'll get clarity of your WHY.

Can my WHY change as I get older?

Our WHY is fully formed by our mid- to late-teens. By that age we've experienced enough and made enough choices of our own that we can recognize the situations in which we'll thrive and those in which we will not. But while you may have sensed your WHY at that age, you probably weren't able to express it. That's because the WHY comes from the limbic part of the brain, which has no capacity for language, so it's hard to put it into words. As years go by, and we gain a deeper understanding of our WHY and the contribution and impact we make, we may find more precise and meaningful language in which to express it. However, the feelings behind the words will stay the same. The words you use may change, but your WHY will not.

If we feel at a certain point in our lives that our WHY has fundamentally changed, there are a few possible reasons.

The most common is that we didn't truly know or understand our WHY before, often because we were too focused on WHATs. Or perhaps we've had an experience that felt transformative—a personal struggle, a tragedy, the death of a loved one. While such events can certainly affect us deeply, they don't change who we are at our core. If these events inspire us to reconsider what's important, to live or think in a more positive way, that doesn't mean our WHY has changed. It means we have gained a deeper understanding of ourselves and have begun to live in closer alignment with our WHY. Another perspective on this is that a challenge or loss can throw us temporarily out of balance. Once we regain our balance, we will see that our WHY is fundamentally the same as it always was.

What if I don't have a WHY?

You do have a WHY. Everyone does. The only question is whether you're willing to let yourself be open and vulnerable enough to discover what it is. As long as you are honest with yourself and others, you *will* discover your WHY. It may not be perfectly articulated or polished right away, but we've never had to break the bad news to someone that they don't have a WHY after all!

The classic bell curve puts early adopters on the left, the majority in the middle, and laggards on the right. WHY follows a similar pattern. Some people are willing and eager to learn their WHY. They believe WHYs exist and are willing to risk a little to discover what theirs is. Others, aren't ready or willing to take the risks involved in discovering what theirs is. In the end, there are sometimes those who, quite frankly, just don't care one way or another. Our goal is not to try to convince the unready or the indifferent. Our goal is to work with those who are inspired by the concept of WHY and have a genuine desire to discover their own.

Can a WHY be bad or evil?

A WHY, by definition, is positive and generative. It serves others and makes a positive contribution to their lives. Those who turn their WHYs to destructive ends have chosen to manifest their purpose, cause or belief through results (WHATs) that hurt, disrespect or otherwise do not serve others. In the thousands of Why Discoveries we've done, we've never had anyone with a Why Statement that implied it could only be used in bad or evil ways. What one does in the name of their WHY is what determines how others view their actions.

What's the reason the WHY is always in service to others?

It comes down to the difference between happiness and fulfillment. Happiness comes from the things we do for ourselves, such as buying a new pair of shoes or the latest smartphone, and can offer a quick hit of dopamine that makes us feel good. But when that feeling wears off, we need to do or buy something else to get the next hit. Shopping (or jogging or drinking wine or sailing or whatever else) may give us fleeting happiness but will never give us lasting fulfillment. The happiness in serving ourselves is real but often fleeting; the fulfillment in serving others is lasting. The problem comes when there's a lack of balance between the pursuit of happiness and the pursuit of fulfillment. That's not just philosophy; it's biology. For more about this, we suggest reading Simon's book *Leaders Eat Last*.

We've met plenty of people over the years who, despite high salaries and the luxurious lifestyles that money can buy, aren't truly fulfilled and feel that there's something missing in their lives. Ironically, people whose WHY is in service to others, rather than for themselves, are the ones who ultimately best serve themselves, because in the end they experience the deepest fulfillment.

How can I make my WHY sound different from everyone else's?

This question stems from the perception that we are all competing and somehow our WHY has to be better than, or at least different from, that of our rivals. But what if the only person we're competing with is ourselves? What if we showed up every day to be a better version of ourselves, living more in line with our own WHY than we did the day before?

When we are truly connected to our WHY and the stories from our past that have led to its discovery, it doesn't matter if our WHY sounds like someone else's. It's ours and it has deep meaning to us. It represents who we are at our very best.

When people first hear about the WHY, they sometimes think we're talking about a person's "special sauce." The WHY is not about finding a competitive advantage. It's okay and not even surprising if all your closest competitors got into the business (whatever it is) for reasons similar to yours. However, even if your WHY is similar to your competitor's, what's likely to be very different is the way you bring it to life through your guiding principles, behaviors and actions (your HOWs). In other words, you're unique, not in your WHY alone but in the combination of your WHY and your HOWs. This combination makes you one-of-a-kind.

If my WHY doesn't align with the work I'm doing, do I have to quit?

We don't *have* to do anything. The short answer to this question is . . . maybe. If your work and your WHY aren't aligning, you don't necessarily have to throw everything away. We can't always control the environment we're in, but we can take responsibility for the way we show up. Your first step should be to positively influence those around you every day. Start by living your WHY the best way you can. It's just possible that, if you do, things will begin to change for the better.

If that doesn't work, it's important to remember that our goal is to surround ourselves with people who believe what we believe. If that simply isn't possible where you are, you have a choice to make. You can actively look for a job that's more in line with your WHY. Or you can try to make the best of where you are. Just remember, moving toward something (e.g., a situation in which you can thrive and live your WHY) is always better than moving away from something (e.g., a situation that isn't working for you).

My boss (or significant other, or sister or best friend) really needs to do a Why Discovery! How can I make that happen?

You're probably right that this person would benefit. However, it's not up to you to convince others. They have to *feel* that Why Discovery would be right for them. One way we can inspire them to do a discovery is to live our own WHY. They may see the fulfillment you find through what you've learned and choose to find out more. Or they may not. We can lead a horse to water and even shove its head in the trough—but that just drowns the horse.

I want to live my WHY but I'm not getting what I need for me to be at my best.

We can't tell from your statement whether you feel your missing piece is tangible or intangible, so we'll give you both answers. The first: if you're implying that there's a tangible WHAT that's necessary for you to live your WHY, you're wrong. None of us needs any specific job, position, title, technology or piece of equipment in order to effect the change we want to see in the world. The Wright brothers, for example, had rivals who were better equipped, better funded and better educated than they were, but the Wrights had passion, and it was their team, working out of a bicycle shop, that launched the first man into the sky in an airplane. There are countless other such stories of people who had far less to work with than others but went on to accomplish things that no one else could. That is what happens when you start with WHY.

But perhaps you are speaking of something intangible— an emotional or relationship need, for instance, that is not being met. Sometimes the people around us don't actually know what we need, which makes it difficult for them to give it to us! If that's the case, you should share your WHY with them and let them know what you need from an emotional or relationship standpoint in order to be at your best.

For Organizations

Do more prestigious or interesting industries have better WHYs than less visible ones? Don't they have better stories to share during the Why Discovery process?

Some people expect that a group specializing in medical or charity work will have more or "better" stories to tell. In our experience, that's not how it works. What binds us together is that we are all human, and the stories you want to draw out during this exercise are about being human. If the people in the session are passionate about what they do, they will almost certainly come up with great stories. *It's the facilitator's job to help. Simply give them enough time and space, listen closely and help them dig deeper.*

What do we do if our product doesn't fit our WHY?

If we sell a product or service that is inconsistent with what we believe, it will be inauthentic, and our employees and customers will eventually see and, more important, *feel* that. On the other hand, to completely change a product or service because it doesn't align with our WHY isn't necessarily a good option either. We've never seen a situation where an organization's entire core business was out of alignment with their WHY. From time to time, a product that isn't doing well or a division that feels like a misfit is now easily explained. We'll hear someone say, "No wonder that's not working; it's out of alignment with our WHY," or "I see the reason this acquisition is struggling; we're out of alignment." Sometimes it makes sense to retire a product or spin off a division that doesn't fit. The idea is to spend energy in places that have the greatest positive impact.

Can a WHY be "to make money"?

No. We all know organizations out there whose sole reason for existing is to make money. But that's not their WHY. "To make money" doesn't fulfill any higher purpose. It's just a result. And organizations that define their WHY as a result tend not to be great places to work. Profit-driven companies may come out financially ahead of WHY-driven organizations in the short term, but their success is unsustainable. Over the long term, they cannot command the kind of loyalty, trust and innovation that an organization with a purpose can.

Costco, for example, has stayed true to its WHY of putting people first, which has served it well. Because Costco has

For more about how WHY is better for the bottom line, read chapter 12 of *Start with Why.*

maintained the clarity of its WHY, it has been both a better place to work and more profitable than its main competitor, the Wal-Mart-owned Sam's Club. After its founder, Sam Walton, died, Wal-Mart's WHY became fuzzy, and management became guided by profit rather than Walton's original WHY. The difference in success between the two companies is clear: if a shareholder had invested in Wal-Mart, Sam's Club's parent company, on the day Walton died, they would have earned a 300 percent return. But if they had invested in Costco the same day, they could have earned an 800 percent gain.

The WHY concept has nothing to do with the reality of business. Don't you have to admit it's a bit fluffy and not how things work in the real world?

For more about the biology of WHY, read chapter 4 of *Start with Why.*

If biology is "fluffy," then consider this fluff! The WHY is at the very heart of business reality. Our decisions are driven by feelings, sometimes (although not always) backed up by logic and reason. When the Dow falls, we often read that "the sentiment of the market" was down. What is "sentiment" if not a feeling? Stocks and shares trade on how those buying them feel about the future.

In 2015, several car manufacturers were found to have falsified their vehicles' emissions testing. Logically enough, that affected people's long-standing trust in those brands, and their sales and market valuations took a tumble. On the other hand, and less logically, Tesla attracted over 500,000 orders for its Model 3 electric car even though it's not yet in production and the people placing the orders have never even sat in a Tesla, let alone driven one.

Our company is large, with many divisions and product lines in several countries. Don't the operational and support functions have different WHYs?

An organization only has one WHY. If some within the organization feel excluded from that WHY, it may be that the Why Statement is not quite there yet—either the words aren't exactly right or the statement still contains WHATs that leave certain employees out. If that's the case, it's probably time to give the Why Statement some thoughtful tweaks.

Or maybe it's time for the company to do some work developing Nested WHYs (page 85). Exploring WHYs within WHYs would give organizational subgroups the opportunity to refine their WHY in a way that resonates more powerfully with them.

Can we adjust our WHY to suit our customers?

During a workshop Peter was running, he heard someone say, "What we need to do is to figure out the WHYs of all our customers and make our WHY match those." Peter's red flag started waving and so should yours if you were to hear something like this.

For more on manipulation vs. inspiration, read chapter 5 of *Start with Why*.

What makes a WHY powerful is its authenticity. Neither employees nor clients are fooled when an organization attempts to manufacture a WHY to suit what they feel customers want to hear. This is manipulation. The people you do business with, and the people who work with you, will sense a disconnect. Trust and loyalty will diminish (if they ever existed). When that happens, the company often resorts to discounts and other forms of manipulation to try to convince customers and employees to stay. This may work in the short term but it has no hope of long-term success.

This is not to say that a WHY-based organization can't use marketing effectively. Of course it can! In fact, when marketing uses the WHY as its source, it works quite well. An organization's branding simply becomes an external expression of its WHY, a proof of the company's culture.

* * *

If you want more inspiration or support, visit the Start with Why website (www.StartWithWhy.com).

Partner Tips for Individual Why Discovery

Anyone who's decided to serve as a partner in a friend or coworker's Individual Why Discovery will want to read chapter 3 of this book for instructions on how to manage the process—and they'll also want this appendix as a cheat sheet. Here is a quick summary of the best tips and questions for being an effective partner.

- **Your role:** Active listener and note taker. As the person going through the discovery tells their stories, you will jot down any recurring ideas, words, phrases and themes. These will eventually constitute a golden thread that defines who the WHY seeker is at their natural best. *Not* **your role:** therapist, mentor, advice giver, problem solver.

- **How to "listen actively":** Make eye contact; show acknowledgment, verbal and nonverbal, of what the other person says; invite them to say more about what happened or how they felt about it. Pay particular attention to facial expressions, body language, long pauses, changes in tone of voice and emotional state (getting excited; getting choked up). Jot these down if you can.

- **Three ways to ask good questions:**

  - **Ask open-ended questions** (i.e., the kind that can't be answered with a "yes" or a "no"). Open-ended questions let the other person lead you.

  - **Avoid questions that start with "why."** It's easier to answer a question that starts with "what." Ask "what is it about that story that really matters to you?"

  - **Sit in silence.** If someone is struggling to answer your question, don't fill the silence with another question or a suggested answer. Just wait. Emotions are hard to articulate and it may take the person a little time to find the right words.

- **Look for silver linings.** A story you hear may be sad or even horrible—but it can still shed light on who someone is and what their WHY might be. Use your outsider perspective to see the lesson that the storyteller may not.

- **Focus on the person's *contribution* and *impact* in each of the stories they tell.** In every story you hear, note *what* the person was giving to someone else and the *impact of what they gave on the recipient*. If the person isn't volunteering that information, ask questions to bring it out.

- **Focus on feelings.** In the stories, *what* happened is less important than how the person *felt* about what happened.

- **Ask questions to dig deeper and uncover feelings.** Here are some effective questions:

  - When that happened, how did it make you feel?

  - Who else was involved in this story and how did they make a difference to you?

  - What is it about this experience that you absolutely loved?

  - You've probably felt this same feeling before. What is it about this particular story that makes it special?

  - How did this experience affect you and who you've become?

  - What was the lesson you learned from that experience that you still carry with you today?

  - Tell me what you meant when you said, "It really filled me up." (Or whatever general statement the storyteller might make.)

- You say what happened made you feel disappointed (or sad or joyful or suspicious). But you've probably felt that way before. Describe how this particular feeling was so different that it still comes to mind all these years later.

- Of all the stories you could have shared with me, what makes this one so special that you chose to tell it as part of your Why Discovery?

EXAMPLE NOTES

Facts	Meaning
• In 2010, facilitated a team off-site in Aspen	• Unity
• Responsible for hiring most of the team over seven years	• Everyone came together
• She knew them all very well, but CEO was there and a lot of the team (remote) hadn't met him yet	• Meant a lot to her that everyone felt like they were in a safe place
• Wasn't sure how it was going to go—nervous	• Team/family feel
• Wanted it to be an experience that brought everyone together	• Joy (everyone was being themselves)
	• Felt a lot of responsibility to the team
	• Loved seeing relationships build naturally
	• Mattered because she truly cared about each person individually

Facilitator Tips for Tribe Why Discovery

Anyone who's agreed to serve as a Tribe Why Discovery facilitator for an organization, company or team will want to read chapters 4 and 5 of this book for instructions on how to manage the process—and they'll also want this appendix as a cheat sheet. Here is a quick summary of the best tips and questions for effective facilitators.

- **Keep it confidential.** Don't share the details or nature of the conversations you will facilitate during the workshop until you're ready to have them. If participants know in advance what they're going to discuss, they'll overthink it.

- **Take a firm hand with "story hogs."** It's crucial to Tribe Why Discovery that everyone gets the opportunity to share their stories in their small group. Keep an eye on the interactions. If some individuals are being too dominant (senior executives are often guilty of this), step up and gently encourage those who haven't yet spoken to contribute their stories.

- **If a team member shows emotion as they report out their story, dig deeper.** Ask the person to say more about their feelings or what it was about that particular story that evoked such an intense reaction. Be direct. Ask, "What was it about that customer's phone call that made you remember it all these years later?"

- **Avoid questions that start with "why."** Counterintuitive as it seems, it's easier to answer a question that starts with "what" or "how."

- **Steer participants away from progress-killing semantic debates.** For example, "Is 'joy' really the best word? I think we should say 'happiness.'" Don't go down that wormhole. Remind the group that, in this context, dictionary definitions matter less than the general feeling a story evokes.

- **Focus participants on *how* their tribe does business, rather than on *what* business they do.** Sometimes group members say that their competition does exactly the same thing they do. If that happens, bring them back to their stories. The difference between them and their competitors lies in the HOW, not the WHAT.

- **Make sure you have enough time.** A Tribe Why Discovery takes at least four hours. If the organizers ask you to do it in less time, push back. Having the full four hours is crucial.

- **Make sure you have the right setting.** The space where the session takes place needs to be:

  - large enough that participants can break into small groups

  - equipped with a snacks table of food and drink

  - private and quiet (e.g., not the room where the Xerox machine is located)

  - set up in advance so that tables are pushed back against the walls and chairs are arranged in a horseshoe

  - supplied with flip charts and easels for each of the subgroups, plus three flip charts on easels for your own use

TRIBE WHY DISCOVERY WORKSHOP

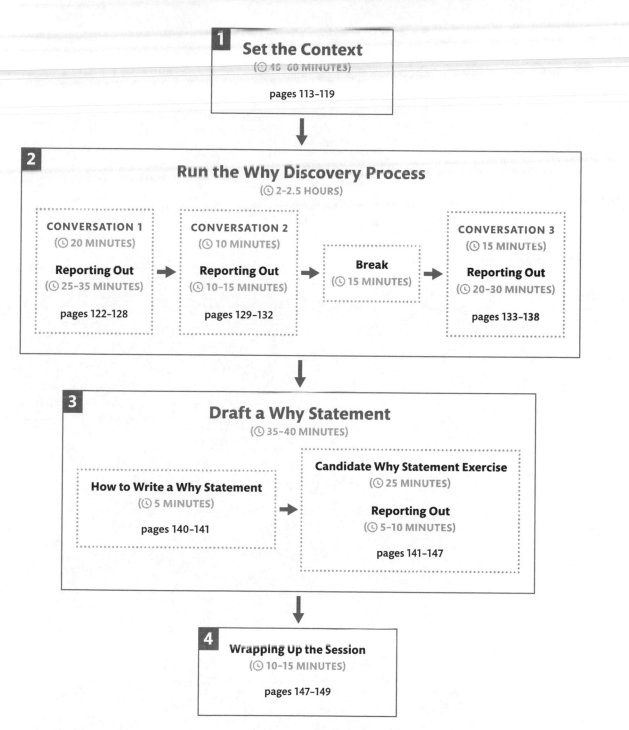

1 **Set the Context**
(⏱ 15–60 MINUTES)

pages 113–119

2 **Run the Why Discovery Process**
(⏱ 2–2.5 HOURS)

CONVERSATION 1
(⏱ 20 MINUTES)

Reporting Out
(⏱ 25–35 MINUTES)

pages 122–128

CONVERSATION 2
(⏱ 10 MINUTES)

Reporting Out
(⏱ 10–15 MINUTES)

pages 129–132

Break
(⏱ 15 MINUTES)

CONVERSATION 3
(⏱ 15 MINUTES)

Reporting Out
(⏱ 20–30 MINUTES)

pages 133–138

3 **Draft a Why Statement**
(⏱ 35–40 MINUTES)

How to Write a Why Statement
(⏱ 5 MINUTES)

pages 140–141

Candidate Why Statement Exercise
(⏱ 25 MINUTES)

Reporting Out
(⏱ 5–10 MINUTES)

pages 141–147

4 **Wrapping Up the Session**
(⏱ 10–15 MINUTES)

pages 147–149

ACKNOWLEDGMENTS

There was a time when we didn't think we'd ever make it to the acknowledgments section of this book! Long story short, this book had started in 2013 as a field guide that Peter had written up. David loved the idea and together we worked to further develop the method. One day we'll pause to reflect on and retrace the steps of how we suddenly found ourselves writing a full-blown book. Writing this book has been an unbelievably challenging and equally inspiring adventure full of unexpected twists and turns.

It would be impossible to name the organizations and individuals that participated in the hundreds of workshops we've conducted to hone the methods we shared in these pages. On the surface it would seem they had nothing in common—different industries, different sizes, different business models—yet they all fit in one bucket to us. They were all early adopters. They were willing to step up and join the movement well before we had this process figured out. If it weren't for you, early adopters, raising your hands to go first, we wouldn't have the content that fills these pages.

A special thanks to all of the organizations who have inspired examples and stories to help bring the Why Discovery processes to life, including La Marzocco, Cuestamoras, Ultimate Software, Studio Awkward and Southwest Airlines. Then there are the numerous individuals who have chatted to us on flights, in bars and other random places, inspiring us by their willingness to share their stories—including Steve the man of steel, Emily and Todd.

With Peter in the UK, David in Utah and Simon in New York, it took some serious effort to bring this book to life. Not to mention that we're all three on the road speaking more than we're at home! A huge thanks to our respective families who have shown great patience, tolerance, love and support as we have each taken ourselves away to write and rewrite—precious time when we already spend many days a year away from home.

Like the instruments in an orchestra, words are nothing without a great arrangement. For that, we thank the skill of the team at Penguin Random House (who between them also helped rid us of a few discordant notes). Adrian Zackheim, Merry Sun, Will Weisser, Victoria Miller, Tara Gilbride, Daniel Lagin, Lisa D'Agostino, Matt Giarratano,

Tess Espinoza and Eric Nelson. Indeed, Portfolio deserves a special mention for their patience and support as we navigated our way through this book.

There are a few others we'd like to mention by name. The wonderfully straight-talking editor Jenn Hallam, who kept us all focused and who never swayed from giving us all the feedback we needed. Judy Coyne, who took three voices and made it one in a way that appeared effortless. Design and layout ideas came from the creative minds of Farah Assir and Elanor Thompson, without whom this guide would have been so much more difficult to follow. A very special thank you to Monique Helstrom and Molly Strong for orchestrating Simon's schedule and our collective logistics to make it possible for us to get in the same room (virtually or in person).

Our ideas and thoughts were shaped by the feedback and input from some close friends and colleagues, including Stephen Shedletzky and the wider Start With Why team, our friends at the Barry-Wehmiller Leadership Institute and Simon Marshall. We want to especially thank all those who spent time and energy testing out what we have written. Ronit Friedman, Sharon Mass and Keren Peled ran a workshop for Elevation Academy, while Margaret Allgood, Aletheia Silcott and Cheryl Grise took Cox Automotive's Inventory Solutions group through the process. Michael Redding and Jeffrey Beruan also played an invaluable part in checking that our process worked.

Finally, we all want to make a special mention of our dear friend Kim Harrison. Kim guides the whole Start With Why team on a daily basis. Without her remarkable vision and insight, her ability to bring people together in the most powerful way and her unwavering commitment to the Start With Why movement, none of this would have been possible. Always in the background, supporting those in the foreground, she is a remarkable human being and we all love her to bits.